# FOUR BLOCKS
## Continued...

## Book II

## Linda Giesler Carlson

Located in Paducah, Kentucky, the American Quilter's Society (AQS), is dedicated to promoting the accomplishments of today's quilters. Through its publications and events, AQS strives to honor today's quiltmakers and their work — and inspire future creativity and innovation in quiltmaking.

EXECUTIVE EDITOR:    JANE R. McCAULEY

EDITOR:    LEAH M. A. DUMORTIER

TECHNICAL EDITOR:    BONNIE K. BROWNING

BOOK DESIGN/ILLUSTRATIONS:    LANETTE BALLARD

COVER DESIGN:    TERRY WILLIAMS

PHOTOGRAPHY:    CHARLES R. LYNCH

**Library of Congress Cataloging-in-Publication Data**

Carlson, Linda Giesler
         Four blocks continued... / by Linda Giesler Carlson
                    p.        cm.
         ISBN 0-89145-795-X
         1. Patchwork--Patterns.  2. Quilting--Patterns.  3. Patchwork
quilts--United States--History.        I. Title.
TT835.C3735        1997
746.46'041--dc21                                                    97-25847
                                                                    CIP

Additional copies of this book may be ordered from: American Quilter's Society,
P.O. Box 3290, Paducah, KY 42002-3290 @ $16.95. Add $2.00 for postage & handling.

# Contents

 *Dedication*

This book is dedicated to:

The keeper of the name, Frederick Parker Giesler, my new nephew;

the giver of the name, Christopher Gustav Nord, my soon to be son-in-law;

and to all the future generations of Nords, Gieslers, Henages, and children of Meredith and Lindsay; grandchildren, grandnieces and nephews, and their children's children.

Some of them may never see me, but they will know me through my legacy of work as the maker and writer of the four-block quilt. May we dream of each other as I dream of those who have gone before me.

 *Preface*

While researching and then upon completion of my first book *Roots, Feathers & Blooms: Four-Block Quilts, Their History & Patterns, Book 1*, by AQS, I was privileged to see many wonderful nineteenth and twentieth century 4-block quilts. Book II will bring some of them to you in updated fabrics, while others stand proudly as historical quilts that shouldn't have new color palettes. I have taken a quilter's license to uncomplicate some of these replicas by making the blocks exactly square, and where necessary, I have made the borders a uniform width. One lovely antique quilt didn't have any two borders exactly alike, and in another I feel quite sure the quiltmaker suddenly realized she would not have the correct width for the last two borders; thereby, she incorporated the selvage into the width of the narrower two borders. Conversely, the appliqué patterns were taken directly from the antique quilts and are therefore, not quite symmetrical. I think the character of the modern quilt should reflect that asymmetrical style.

Since the first book was published in 1994, quilters and quilt dealers contact me regularly about 4- to 6-block quilts, Pennsylvania maintaining the highest number of these quilts, frequently of German heritage.

A special thanks of appreciation to Marilyn Woodin of Woodin Wheel Antiques in Kalona, IA, for always finding great quilts for me! Her knowledge and integrity are impeccable, and her friendship is a treasure to me. Also, to Alicelee Graf of The Antique Quilt Source in Carlisle, PA, who came to hear my paper, "The Roots of the Large Four-Block Quilt" given at the symposium, "What's American About the American Quilt?" at the Smithsonian Institute in 1995. Since then, she has found the 4-block Eagle quilt and Gordian Knot featured in this book. Both dealers have my wholehearted recommendation.

I also want to thank Sara Miller and her staff at Kalona Kountry Kreations in Kalona, Iowa, for providing me with an artist's palette of fabrics. Her shop is the pot of gold at the end of the rainbow!

*Four Blocks Continued...*

# General Supplies and Directions

The following supplies and directions are detailed here and therefore should be considered for all pattern instructions.

## Basic Sewing Kit

¹⁄₁₆" hole punch
template plastic
paper and fabric scissors
#10 or #11 appliqué needles (sharps)
quilting needles
thimble
thread to match appliquéd fabric
thread for blocks, borders, and binding
fabric markers
backing fabric
batting
sewing machine

## Fabrics

Prewash and iron *all* fabrics before using to guard against any color bleeding.

## Template Patterns

All template patterns, except for those that are machine pieced, *do not* have seam allowances included. You will need to cut the patterns, about ⅛" away, from your traced line on the fabric.

**Machine pieced pieces:** Use an accurate ¼" seam allowance guide. For the Mariner's Compass, a seam allowance is included on the patterns. My secret to accurate machine piecing is to use a ¹⁄₁₆" hole punch to mark the sewing line in the seam allowance on the template plastic. Just remember to place a dot inside each hole when tracing around them on the fabric. These dots are the pinning and sewing line guides.

## Dogtooth Squares

Step 1: Match the two fabrics with right sides together and raw edges perfectly matched. (Yardage requirements are given in the pattern directions.)

Step 2: Draw a grid of squares, as per pattern directions (Fig. 1).

Step 3: Draw diagonal lines through each grid square (Fig. 2).

Step 4: Sew accurately ¼" away from both sides of the diagonal lines. Pick up the foot at each horizontal line, cut your threads, and start again on the next diagonal line (Fig. 3).

Step 5: When each square has been sewn on both sides of the diagonal lines, cut the squares apart on all drawn lines: horizontal, diagonal, and vertical (Fig. 4). Lightly press the Dogteeth open.

Step 6: Using a ¼" seam, sew the number of squares together as indicated in the pattern directions. Be sure to have the Dogtooth colors alternate (Fig. 5).

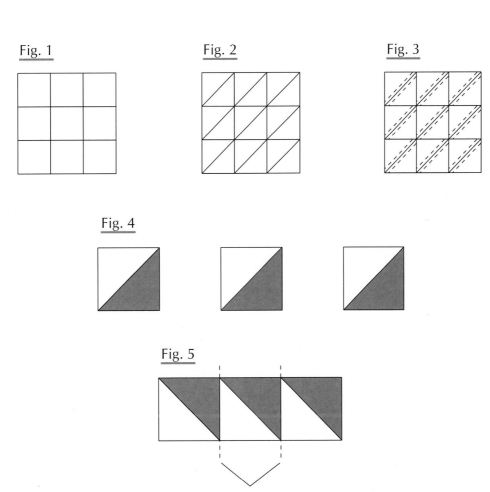

Fig. 1

Fig. 2

Fig. 3

Fig. 4

Fig. 5

seam lines

*Four Blocks Continued...*

## Flying Geese Squares

Step 1: Cut the number of Unit 1's and Unit 2's as indicated in the pattern instructions.

Step 2: With right sides together, pin two Unit 2's (background squares) on the Unit 1 (Fig. 1).

Step 3: With a ruler, draw a diagonal line through the Unit 2's (Fig. 2).

Step 4: On both sides of the diagonal line, stitch an accurate ¼" seam (Fig. 2).

Step 5: Cut apart on the diagonal line. This forms two pieces (Fig. 3).

Step 6: Take one of the new pieces. Finger press or iron the Unit 2's with their seam allowances away from the Unit 1's (Fig. 4).

Step 7: Pin with right sides together another Unit 2 to the lower right angle corner of the Unit 1 (Fig. 5).

Step 8: Draw a diagonal line through the new Unit 2 (Fig. 5).

Step 9: Stitch ¼" away from both sides of the diagonal line. Cut apart on the diagonal line. Finger press open. Two finished Flying Geese units are formed (Fig. 6).

Step 10: Repeat with remaining units.

Step 11: Join the number of flying geese units as indicated in the pattern instructions (Fig. 7).

*The directions for the machine pieced Flying Geese are reprinted courtesy of Ken and Shirley Wengler, Newberry, FL.*

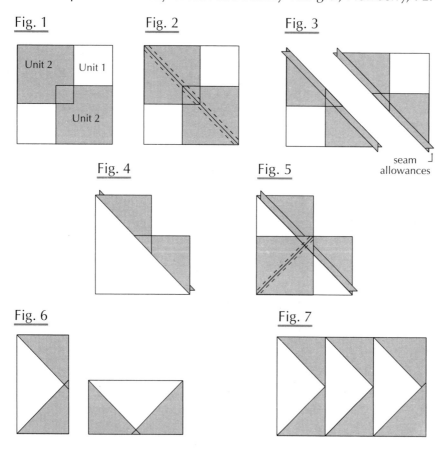

## *Machine Applied Binding*

Self-made or purchased binding may be used. I prefer a straight grain, double-fold binding made from one of the fabrics in the quilt because it gives a clean, crisp edge. To make the binding, cut 2¼" wide strips; sew end to end, then fold the entire length in half, wrong sides together, and press.

Applying the binding: On the right side of the finished quilt, about 6" away from a corner, place and pin raw edges of binding against raw edge of quilt (Fig. 1). Fold the beginning edge of the binding up to form a 45° angle. Begin stitching, stopping ¼" away from the corner. Backstitch to secure threads, then cut them. Lift the machine foot to reposition quilt before continuing to next corner (Fig. 2).

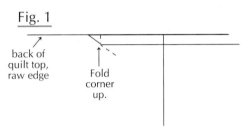

Fig. 1

back of quilt top, raw edge — Fold corner up.

Now, lift and fold the loose end of the binding to a 45° angle (Fig. 3). Next, fold the binding back down over the folded angle so that the second fold is even with the edge of the quilt. Pin to the side of the quilt (Fig. 4).

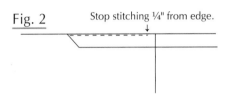

Fig. 2    Stop stitching ¼" from edge.

Position the needle back into the ¼" tacking; take two stitches, then backstitch, before continuing in the same manner down the remaining sides and corners. Repeat procedure for each corner.

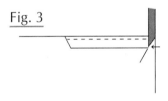

Fig. 3

Overlap the binding and stitch a couple of inches past the beginning. Fold binding over to the back side of the quilt and stitch in place by hand.

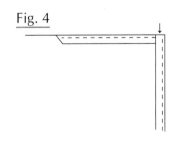

Fig. 4

*Four Blocks Continued...*

# Coxcomb Crossing
### 112" x 112"

This large block was inspired by an antique multi-block quilt owned by the Audrain County Historical Society Museum in Mexico, MO. It was donated by Miss Virginia Botts, whose ancestors came from Kentucky. A very similar quilt was found by the Kentucky Quilt Project. I have named it "Coxcomb Crossing" as it has previously been called "Unknown" by Barbara Brackman, author of Encyclopedia of Appliqué. Made by the author, 1994.

# Coxcomb Crossing

## Supplies

Basic sewing kit, page 6
Compass
Batting for 112" square
Backing for 112" square

## Fabric Requirements

11¾ yds. white for background and borders
2 yds. green
3 yds. red
2½ yds. pink
½ yd. yellow
2¼ yds. floral print
⅛ yd. dark green
¾ yd. binding

42" Coxcomb Crossing block

## Cutting Instructions (Patterns, page 69)

Instructions on the pattern pieces are for one block, unless otherwise noted.

Cut (4) 42½" squares for blocks
Cut (2) 14½" x 84½" borders
Cut (2) 14½" x 112½" borders
Cut (4) yellow A
Cut (16) red B
Cut (32) green and (32) pink C
Cut (32) green and (32) pink Cr
Cut (16) green D
Cut (16) green E
Cut (16) yellow F
Cut (80) pink and (18) red G
Cut (64) red and (18) pink H
Cut (98) red I
Cut (16) red I-a and (16) red I-ar

Cut (16) white J and (16) white Jr
Cut (16) green K and (16) green Kr
Cut (16) white L and (16) white Lr
Cut (16) green M and (16) green Mr
Cut (16) white N and (16) white Nr
Cut (16) white O
Cut (44) floral P
Cut (12) dark green Q
Cut (4) pink and (4) red R
Cut (4) red S
Cut (4) floral T
Cut (4) green and (4) dark green U
Cut (1) floral 6" circle
•See center appliqué, step 1, pg. 17

Cut and make 2¼" x 455" (eleven 2¼" x 44" strips) white binding.

Trace all templates on the wrong side of fabric, *except for P through U*. Add ¼" seam allowance to all pieces.

Join five P's end to end eight times to make the border appliqués.

*Four Blocks Continued...*

## Block Assembly

Step 1: Sew crossing section of block. Piece Unit 1 by sewing a B to each side of A (Fig. 1).

Step 2: Make four Unit 2's by first piecing 16 sets of one green C and one pink C triangles to form individual rectangles. Repeat for Cr green and Cr pink triangles (Fig. 2).

Step 3: Sew two rectangles, short ends together. Keep C rectangles separate from Cr rectangles (Fig. 3).

Step 4: Sew stem D to a pair of C rectangles. Repeat with remaining three pairs of C rectangles (Fig. 4).

Step 5: Sew Cr rectangle pairs to other side of D stem units (Fig. 5).

Step 6: For top row of inner Crossing block, sew an O piece to each side of a Unit 2, noting the unit's direction (Fig. 6).

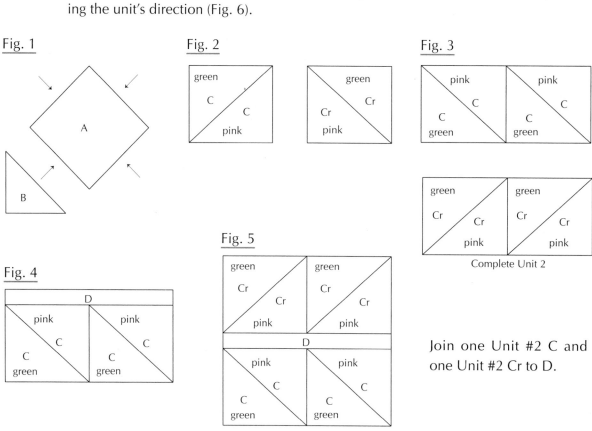

Fig. 1

Fig. 2

Fig. 3

Complete Unit 2

Fig. 4

Fig. 5

Join one Unit #2 C and one Unit #2 Cr to D.

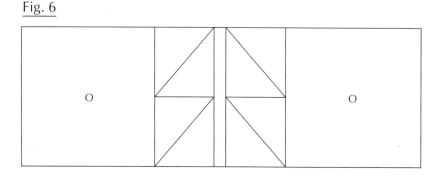

Fig. 6

Step 7: To complete middle row, sew two Unit 2's to each side of a Unit 1, noting opposing directions of the Unit 2's (Fig. 7).

Step 8: Sew the bottom row the same as the top row, but reverse the direction of Unit 2 (Fig. 8).

Step 9: Join the top row to the middle row, abutting seam allowances of units. Then add to bottom row in same manner. Set aside this inner crossing section.

Step 10: To piece the Coxcomb sections, first separate fabric pieces and the reverse pieces. For the leaf section, Unit 3, sew J to K, then add L. Repeat for Jr, Kr, Lr. Continue in same manner for three remaining flowers (Fig. 9).

Step 11: Sew short stem E to J,K,L, then join the Jr, Kr, Lr section. Repeat for the other three flowers (Fig. 10).

Fig. 7

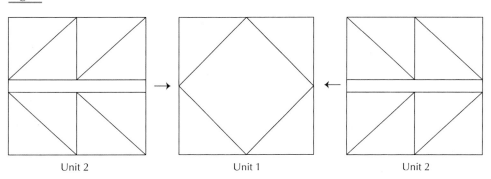

Unit 2      Unit 1      Unit 2

Fig. 8

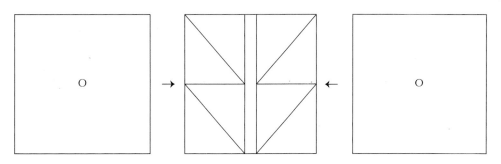

O      O

Fig. 9      Fig. 10

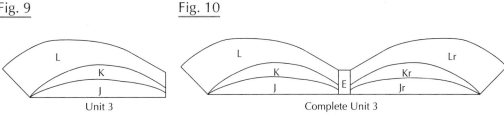

Unit 3      Complete Unit 3

*Four Blocks Continued...*

## Coxcomb Section

**Step 12:** Piece F must be set into Unit 3 by first sewing the flat bottom to the top of E. Attach F's bias sides to L by starting at the corners of E and sewing towards the top arch of F (Fig. 11).

**Step 13:** Sew three I's to three G's, one I-a to one G, and one I-ar to one G for each of the four flowers. (Hint: pin the beginning and end of pieces, then in the middle distributing fullness evenly. Clip only if necessary to ease curve.) Add H to one side of G – I section; then attach another G – I section to the H just sewn. Sew the two I's from their inner corners outward (Fig. 12).

**Step 14:** Continue adding H's to G – I sections on both sides of the center G – I section of the Coxcomb until the flower has four H's and five G – I's.

**Step 15:** Sew M to N. Repeat for Mr and Nr, and remaining three flowers.

**Step 16:** Attach M – N and Mr – Nr sections to the ends of the Coxcombs starting at bottom of first and last G's and sewing outward (Fig. 13).

Fig. 11

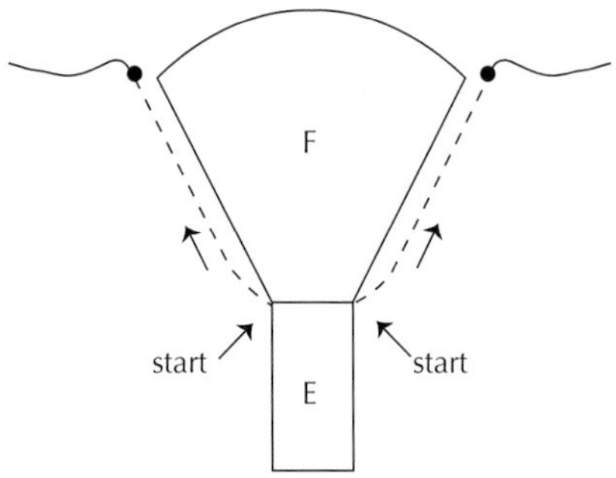

Fig. 12

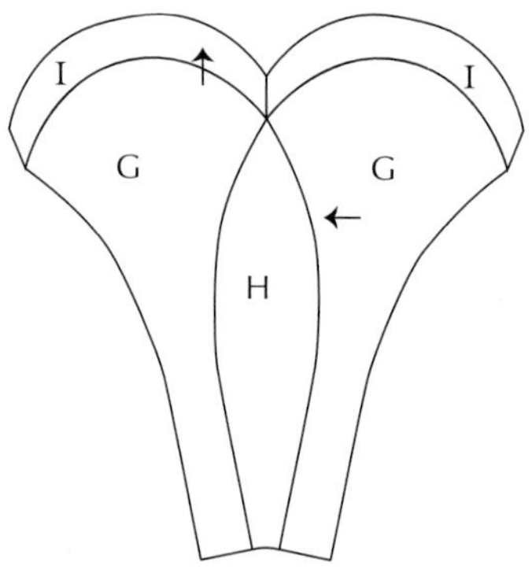

Unit 4

Fig. 13

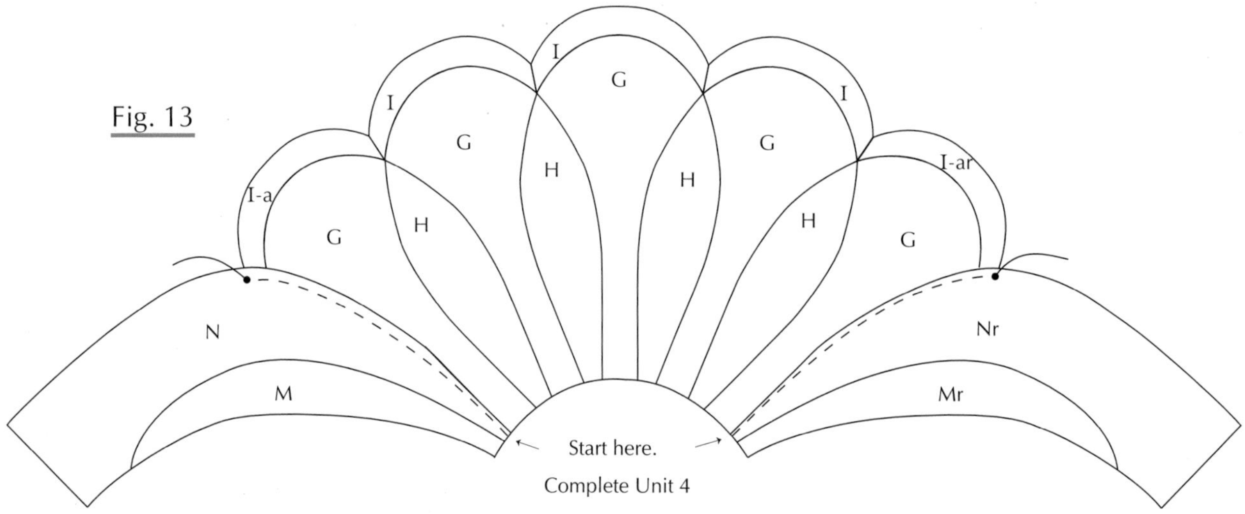

Start here.
Complete Unit 4

Step 17: Sew leaf, Unit 3, to Coxcomb, Unit 4. The yellow center F will be pinned and sewn first. Starting where the inner edge of Lr meets Mr, pin F piece of Unit 3 to Unit 4, ending with M being even with the curved edge of F. Ease, if necessary, and sew (Fig. 14a). Sew remaining parts of Units 3 and 4 by starting at outer corner of F, pinning L to M and sewing outward (Fig. 14b). Repeat at beginning corner of F for attaching Lr to Mr. Complete remaining flowers in the same manner.

Fig. 14 a & b

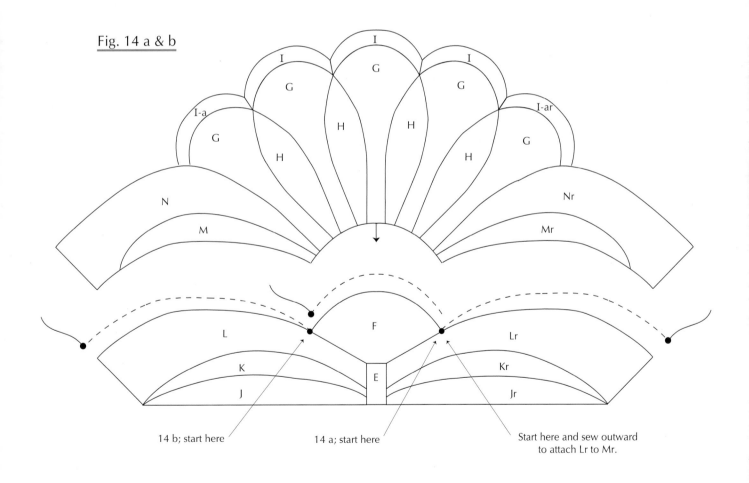

14 b; start here

14 a; start here

Start here and sew outward to attach Lr to Mr.

*Four Blocks Continued . . .*

Step 18: Sew Coxcombs to Inner Crossing. Sew bottoms of Unit 3's to four sides of inner Crossing section. Attach diagonal edges of LMN to adjacent Coxcomb by starting at inner corner of block and sewing outward. Repeat for all corners, see below. Center and pin the block onto 42½" square background. Turn under on pencil lines of I, N, and Nr pieces and appliqué all edges down. Turn over and carefully cut back of block ¼" – ½" away from appliqué stitching on back.

Step 19: Join all four blocks.

## Coxcomb Crossing Corner

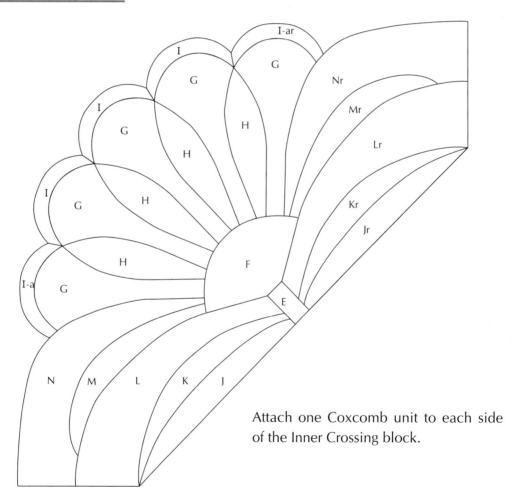

Attach one Coxcomb unit to each side of the Inner Crossing block.

# Coxcomb Crossing

## Center Appliqué

Step 1: Draw a circle using the compass, 5½" in diameter on the right side of the floral fabric. This will be the sewing line. Enlarge the compass to 6". Make another circle around the first. This will give an accurate ¼" seam allowance for appliquéing over the bases of the G–H–I units.

Step 2: Match and pin I to G (Fig. 15). Distribute the fullness evenly. Clip only if necessary to ease curve. Sew. Repeat for all 18 units.

Step 3: Add H to one side of the G–I unit. Attach another G–I unit to the first H. Sew both I's from the inner corner outward (Fig. 15).

Step 4: Continue adding H's to the other G–I units. Join each I until all 18 form a circle.

Step 5: Flatten the circle on an ironing board. Iron on a low setting, barely pressing, if necessary. Hot ironing could stretch the motif.

Step 6: Center the 5½" circle over the G–H–I unit. Needle turn under the edges and appliqué in place.

Step 7: Center the completed motif over the quilt center. Pin and needle turn appliqué in place leaving ½" to ¾" open over each seam line for the branches to be inserted.

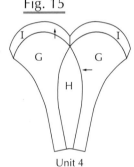

Fig. 15

Unit 4

Step 8: Reverse appliqué a scrap piece of material under four Q's. Place and pin the four P's in each of the center motif openings. Pattern reference, Fig. 16.

Step 9: Pin and appliqué the complete Q's under the top end of the branches. Place two R's, one red and one pink, beside Q and appliqué. Appliqué the branch in place. Repeat for remaining branches.

## Borders

The borders should be appliquéd before being attached.

Step 1: Find the center of each border by folding horizontally and vertically. Iron lightly.

Step 2: Appliqué the curved top edge of T onto S. Pattern reference, Fig. 17. Baste the bottom of T to S. Repeat for remaining units.

Step 3: Center and pin the end petals of the T–S unit over the center of each border. Pin a long branch (5P's) on the border's vertical pressed line with their ends tucked under the T–S side petals. Pattern reference, Fig. 17. Appliqué branch in place leaving the outer end of the branch open.

Step 4: Appliqué T–S in place except bottom edges. Pin two U's, a green and a dark green, to bottom edge of T–S unit. Appliqué in place.

Step 5: Repeat for remaining borders.

Step 6: Center and pin the 14½" x 84½" border to the top of the quilt. Sew. Repeat for bottom border. Center each 14½" x 112½" side borders. Sew.

Four Blocks Continued...

## Quilting Instructions

Layer backing, batting, and top. Baste. Quilt as desired.
Apply 2¼" x 455" (eleven – 2¼" x 44" strips ) binding as per general instructions, page 9.

Fig. 16

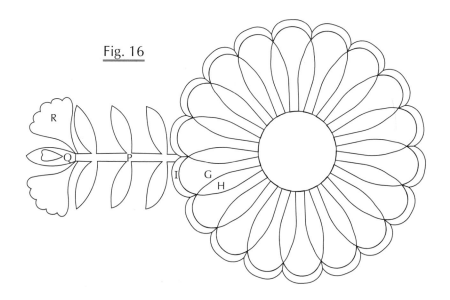

Fig. 17

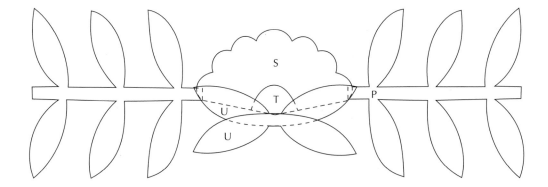

## Coxcomb Crossing Block

# Oak Leaf & Reel with Tulips
## 82½" x 82½"

Oak leaves, reels, and tulips were combined in this traditional red and white antique quilt. Made in Pennsylvania, c. 1880s.

This modern version by the author uses a checked background, plaid flowers, and a gold print, resulting in a homespun — style quilt. 1996.

# Oak Leaf & Reel with Tulips

The traditional colors of red and white or homespun-like fabrics may be used. This pattern gives directions for a homespun-style quilt. For a two-color quilt, use and cut templates from the same color for both primary and secondary fabric/cutting requirements.

## Supplies

Basic sewing kit, page 6
Batting for 82½" square
Backing for 82½" square

34" Oak Leaf & Reel with Tulips block

## Fabric Requirements

6¾ yds. for background, borders, sashing, and binding
2 yds. primary color – gold print
2 yds. secondary color – plaid

## Cutting Instructions *(Patterns, page 75)*

Instructions on the pattern pieces are for one block, unless otherwise noted.

Cut (4) 34½" blocks of background fabric
Cut (2) 6½" x 71" borders
Cut (2) 6½" x 83" borders
Cut (4) 3" x 34½" sashes
Cut straight grain strips to equal
2¼" x 335" (eight 2¼" x 44") for binding

| Primary color | Secondary color |
|---|---|
| Cut (4) A | Cut (16) B |
| Cut (16) C | Cut (48) D |
| Cut (48) G | Cut (16) E |
| Cut (6) L | Cut (32) F |
| Cut (6) Lr | Cut (174) H |
| Cut (22) N | Cut (16) I |
| | Cut (16) J |
| | Cut (16) K |
| | Cut (4) L |
| | Cut (4) Lr |
| | Cut (1) M |
| | Cut (26) O |

Trace and cut out each template. Trace the A template, flipping to make all four corners, on paper then transfer to template plastic and cut as one piece.

## Block Assembly

Step 1: Trace all appliqués on the right side of the fabric. Cut out about ⅛" away from the lines, *except for M,* for seam allowance.

*Four Blocks Continued...*

Step 2: Fold one 34½" background block in half horizontally, vertically, and diagonally. Lightly press and open.

Step 3: Center A over the center of the block aligning leaves with the diagonal creases. Pin or loosely baste through the diagonal (Fig. 1).

Step 4: Slip four B reels under the A's (Fig. 2). Loosely baste. Pin four C's under the four reels (Fig. 2).

Step 5: Using matching thread, needle turn under the seam allowance on the leaves and appliqué down. Repeat for reel edges. Appliqué the oak leaves in place last.

Step 6: Position and pin the corner flower stems so that the long center stem E is on top of the two F's (Fig. 3). Make 4 E–F–F units.

Step 7: Pin I's over the E bases and match the entire unit in the corner of the block, raw edges of the block matched to the I right angle. Appliqué the three stems. Baste the right angle edges of the triangle to the block.

Step 8: Center, pin, and stitch the G's on the D's (Fig. 4). Make 12.

Step 9: Place and sew complete G–D unit on each appliquéd stem (Fig. 5).

Step 10: Pin and sew two H's on the two outside F's and two H's on the center E stem (Fig 3).

Step 11: Repeat steps 6–10 for each corner.

Step 12: Between each of the four corner flower clusters, center K, lining each up with its C leaf. Appliqué in place.

Step 13: Pin J over each K with the center petal pointing directly at the C leaf. Appliqué. Add two H's to the tulip stems and appliqué.

Repeat steps for each block.

Fig. 1

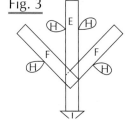

Fig. 2

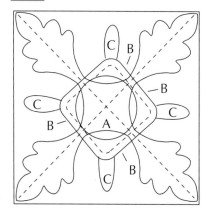

Fig. 5

Fig. 3

Fig. 4

## Sashing

Appliqué three primary color L's and two secondary color L's to each of the four sashes. Pay close attention to the direction of the leaves. They should point towards M when the sashes are attached to the blocks.

Sew a sash between the top two blocks with the sash leaves pointing down (Fig. 6).

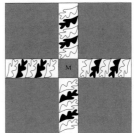

Fig. 6

Sew a second sash to M. Attach a third sash directly opposite. Remember to always have the leaves pointing towards the center.

Sew the sash – square – sash unit to the base of the two joined blocks by matching up the seam lines (Fig. 6).

Sew the fourth sash between the remaining two blocks. Join all four blocks; again match sash seam lines.

## Borders

To correctly position the appliqués on the 6½" x 71" top and bottom borders, fold the borders in half to find the center. Finger press the fold. Open. Center N over this crease. The remaining swags and O's can now be positioned equally.

Appliqué swags first, then tassels.

Pin three H's over the bottom of each tassel. Appliqué the two side leaves first. Position the center leaf over the bases of the side leaves. Appliqué in place. Sew top and bottom borders to the quilt.

Find the center of the 6½" x 83" side borders by folding and finger pressing. Center O over the crease. Position the remaining swags and tassels equally.

Appliqué swags, tassels, and leaves as done for the top and bottom borders.

Sew side borders to the quilt.

## Finishing

Layer backing, batting, and top. Baste. Quilt as desired. Apply binding following the general directions, page 9.

*Four Blocks Continued...*

# Amish Rose of Sharon Wreath — An Ode to Sara Miller

84" x 84"

Rose of Sharon Wreath, made by Emma Barrett in Anson County, NC, c. 1850.

This Amish version of the Rose of Sharon Wreath, made by the author, is a tribute to Sara Miller, Kalona, Iowa. 1997.

# Amish Rose of Sharon Wreath

## Supplies

Basic sewing kit, page 6
Backing for 84" block
Batting for 84" block
Sewing machine

## Fabric Requirements*

4½ yds. dark green
2½ yds. red
2½ yds. bright red
2¼ yds. medium green
¾ yd. red stripe
¾ yd. red for binding
¼ yd. pink
¼ yd. gold
½ yd. light green

30" Amish Rose of Sharon Wreath block

*Colors given are for a traditional Amish color palette.

## Cutting Instructions (Patterns, page 80)

Instructions on the pattern pieces are for one block, unless otherwise noted.

Cut (4) 30½" dark green blocks
Cut (2) 8½" x 68½" red borders
Cut (2) 8½" x 84½" red borders
Cut 2¼" x 345" bright red straight grain binding
Cut (4) red stripe A
Cut (4) pink B
Cut (3) gold C
Cut (1) gold D
Cut (32) medium green E
Cut (16) red F

Cut (16) gold G
Cut (16) medium green H
Cut (16) medium green Hr
Cut (16) light green I
Cut (16) light green Ir
Cut (16) med. green J
Cut (16) med. green Jr
Cut (32) med. green K
Cut (32) med. green Kr
Cut (80) red stripe L
Cut (40) red L
Cut (40) bright red L

Trace all templates on the right side of the fabric. Leave a ⅛" seam allowance.

Four Blocks Continued...

Fig. 1

# Block Assembly

Step 1:  Fold a 30½" x 30½" block into quarters to find the center. Finger press.

Step 2:  Center and pin A over the center and align it with the four folds.

Step 3:  Insert eight E's under the convex petals. Appliqué these first, then the (A) rose.

Step 4:  On the back of the block, carefully cut out the back of the block ¼" inside the appliqué stitches to facilitate quilting later on.

Step 5:  Place and pin the B over A. Appliqué in place. Cut out the back again leaving a ¼" seam allowance.

Step 6:  Place C on the B rose. Appliqué in place. Do not cut this one out. Substitute D for C on last block.

Step 7:  Notice how the corner roses (F) are placed in the blocks shown above. Measure diagonally from the corner edge 3¼" and pin F there.

Step 8:  Insert G rose center for reverse appliqué and pin. Place the J and Jr stems in the correct positions. Pin in place the K and Kr rose leaves. Loosely baste with long running stitches down the piece center. Remove all pins.

Step 9:  Pin the H and Hr leaves and the I and Ir pods on each side of the corner rose. Match the pod tip to the mark on the leaf. Template instructions, page 6. The leaf will be appliquéd over the bottom curve of the pod. Loosely baste the leaves and the pods. Appliqué them to the block.

Step 10: Pin five L cherries above each H–I unit.
Appliqué in place.

Repeat steps for each block. Join the four blocks (Fig. 1).

## Flying Geese Inner Border

Make 148 geese units.
Cut (37) 5¼" x 5¼" bright red square unit 1's.
Cut (74) 2⅞" x 2⅞" dark green unit 2's.

Follow assembly instructions on page 8.

Once the Flying Geese squares have been completed, sew 30 Flying Geese units together so that they are all pointing the same direction. Attach this band to one side of the quilt top by matching the center of the Flying Geese band to the quilt center seam. Pin outward. Sew using a ¼" seam allowance on the sewing machine. Repeat for the other side only have the geese flying the opposite direction.

Sew 32 Flying Geese units together for the top inner border. Match and pin from the center outwards. Be sure the direction of the geese units continues the direction of the side borders, not reverses it (Fig. 1).

Sew with ¼" allowance.

Repeat for the bottom border. Remember to check the geese direction.

## Outer Borders

Fold a 8½" x 68½" red border to find the center. Finger press. Match fold to the quilt side center seam. Pin outwards. Sew.

Repeat for the opposite side border.

Fold to find the center of the 8½" x 84½" top and bottom borders. Pin from the center seam outwards. Sew.

## Quilting Instructions

Mark the quilt top with quilting lines as desired. Layer the batting, backing, and top. Baste. Quilt closely and consistently, a hallmark of Amish quilts.

Make and attach 2¼" x 345" (eight 2¼" x 44" strips) bright red binding, general instructions, page 9.

*Four Blocks Continued...*

# Monet's Midnight Garden for Diana
## 72" x 72"

This watercolor quilt has four 21" x 21" blocks made up of 2¼" squares and triangles with an overlayed appliquéd tree. The multicolored squares symbolize a moonlit, star-filled sky over a magically living root and bulb filled earth. Made by the author, 1996, for her twin sister Diana's forty-something birthday.

# Monet's Midnight Garden for Diana

**Before you begin.** Consult books and magazines featuring watercolor quilts. Remember a Kaleidoscope's color formation. Decide if you want your borders and blocks to be the same or symbolically different. Choose your fabric accordingly.

## Supplies

Basic sewing kit, page 6
1 yd. x 1 yd. flannel or flannel backed cloth for design layout
Colored pencils or felt watercolor pens
Four 24" x 24" 1" graph paper sheets
Ruler
Rotary cutter
Sewing machine
Appliqué needle
Matching appliqué thread
Neutral machine thread
Embroidery beads & floss (optional)

72" x 72"
Monet's Midnight Garden for Diana

## Fabric Requirements

2 yds. for tree
1½ yds. for inner borders*
2½ yds. for outer borders and binding*
72" x 72" backing
72" x 72" batting
Scrap fabric for bulbs
Assorted 2½" squares and triangles, 400 are required for background
*Yardages given for borders cut from the same fabric.

**Fabric choice.** Cloth printed with small flowers should be positioned in the foreground. Tall flower prints would go toward the middle to back of the block. Some of the tree fabric gives depth perception if used in the back of the block. Mottled or faux suede fabrics make wonderful skies or breaks between flowers. Add a few drab colors in the flower beds to make the flowers stand out.

*Four Blocks Continued...*

## Template Assembly

**Remember:** Trace all templates on the right side of the fabric. Cut out ⅛" away for seam allowance on tree.

Enlarge the tree design on page 85 to make a full-size pattern. Cut out the pattern and trace onto tree fabric.

## Cutting Instructions *(Patterns, page 84)*

Instructions on the pattern pieces are for one block, unless otherwise noted.

Cut (2) 5½" x 42½" top/bottom inner borders
Cut (2) 5½" x 52½" side inner borders
Cut (2) 10½" x 52½" top/bottom outer borders
Cut (2) 10½" x 72½" side outer borders
Cut (400) 2¼" A squares and B triangles (seam allowance is included)
Cut C, D, and E bulbs as needed
Make 2¼" x 300" (seven 2¼" x 44" strips) binding

## Block Assembly

Step 1: Cut six A squares and six B triangles from six different fabrics. Be certain when cutting out floral fabric that the flowers are perpendicular to the point (Fig. 1). On the 24" x 24" graph paper, beginning 1¾" from the lower right corner, lay out some squares and triangles (Fig. 2).

Step 2: Using colored pencils or markers, color in some blocks on the graph paper to get a general color coordinated image. Viewing the four paper blocks together on a light colored board helps to visualize the final effect (Fig. 3).

<u>Fig. 1</u>

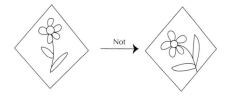

Not →

<u>Fig. 2</u>

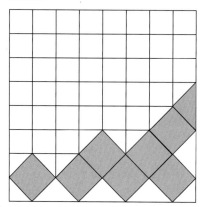

Step 3: Once the color pattern has been chosen, cut the appropriate number of squares and triangles of each color. Each block has 49 squares and 28 triangles.

Fig. 3

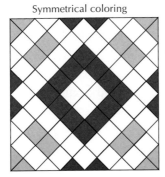

Symmetrical coloring

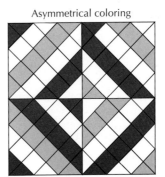

Asymmetrical coloring

**Quilter's tip:** Use a ruler and rotary cutter to mark and cut 2¼" wide strips. Cut the strips into 2¼" squares. Mark and cut the triangles, as needed, on the wrong side of the fabric.

Step 4: Place the squares according to the colored design on the flannel cloth which will hold the pieces in place without pins.

Step 5: When satisfied with their placement, start sewing the squares together beginning with the middle diagonal row. Start at one corner and sew the triangle to the square placed diagonally next to it. Lightly press seams all in the same direction.

Step 6: Sew row 2 together in the same way. Press the seams in the opposite direction (Fig. 4).

Step 7: Join row 1 to row 2.

Step 8: Repeat, forming each row and joining to the previous, until one half of the block is completed. Make the second half likewise. Join the halves and lightly press.

Step 9: Repeat assembly for remaining three blocks.

Fig. 4

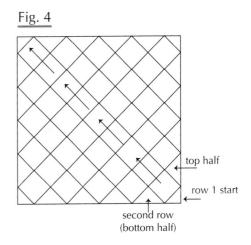

top half

row 1 start

second row
(bottom half)

31

*Four Blocks Continued...*

## Joining the Blocks

Join the top two blocks, then the bottom two. Join bottom half to the top half matching and pinning outwards from the center seam. Sew.

## Borders

Fold in half to find the center of the 5½" x 42½" top inner border. Match to center seam and pin outwards. Sew. Repeat for bottom inner border.

Center, pin, and sew the 5½" x 52½" side inner borders in the same manner.

Repeat process for the outer borders. Attach the top and bottom, 10½" x 52½", borders first, then the sides, 10½" x 72½".

## Appliqués

Appliqué as many of the C, D, and E bulbs as desired. A small piece of batting underneath makes them really stand out. Stems may be freehand cut and needle turn appliquéd. Roots can be added with a random embroidery stitch.

Place the tree over the quilt surface. Loosely baste in place. Needle turn the edges and appliqué.

**Option:** Sew beads with embroidery floss to represent fireflies or stars.

## Finishing

Layer backing, batting and top. Quilt as desired.

**Suggestion:** quilt lines to accentuate the patterns in the fabric.

Outline quilt the tree and bulbs.

**Suggestion:** quilt individual squares (Fig. 5).

Apply binding following the general directions, page 9.

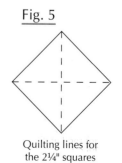

Fig. 5

Quilting lines for
the 2¼" squares

# 1830 Mennonite Rose Wreath
## 89" x 89"

Made in Lancaster, PA, c. 1830, this Mennonite quilt's colors have not dimmed. The cheddar orange still blazes; the rich brown is not brittle. The unfaded green print accented by yellow and blue sprigs and black outlines shows no trace of wear. Indications of the maker's German heritage are evidenced by the orange background and pieced inner border.

# 1830 Mennonite Rose Wreath

The pattern given here resembles the English "President's Wreath" of red, green, and white coloration with appliquéd yellow flower centers.

## Supplies

Basic sewing kit, page 6
Batting for 89" square
Backing for 89" square
Sewing machine

30" Rose Wreath block

## Fabric Requirements

6 yds. orange for background and flower centers
3⅜ yds. green print for leaves, stems, and Dogtooth squares
2¾ yds. brown for flowers, binding, and Dogtooth squares

## Cutting Instructions (Patterns, page 86)

Instructions on the pattern pieces are for one block, unless otherwise indicated.

Cut (4) orange 30½" blocks
Cut (2) orange 12½" x 65½" borders
Cut (2) orange 12½" x 89½" borders
Cut (29) 5½" brown A
Cut (24) green B
Cut (48) green C
Cut (24) green D
Cut (24) brown E
Cut (192) green F
Cut (29) orange G

Trace all templates on the right side of the fabric.

## Block Assembly

Step 1: Fold the 30½" x 30½" block in half horizontally and vertically to find the center. Finger press. Starting with A, place it first then the six other roses around it. Pin temporarily. Position the orange center G on each rose.

Step 2: Insert six B's between the roses to form a balanced circle. The diameter of the circle should be about 18". Once satisfied with the placement, loosely baste a running stitch through the middle of the rose wreath to eliminate the number of pins.

Step 3: Pin 12 C's and six D's with the six E's as shown. Pattern reference, page 34. Balance their placement. Add the F's and baste with a running stitch. *The leaves are not inserted under the stems; they just meet the edges.*

Step 4: Appliqué the entire block. Repeat for the remaining three blocks. Join the four blocks.

Step 5: Appliqué the last A rose over the center.

## Dogtooth Borders

Using the following requirements, follow instructions for making Dogtooth Squares on page 7.

Make 100 Dogtooth squares.

Cut 1 yd. of brown.
Cut 1 yd. of green print.
Draw a grid of 3⅜" squares, 12 rows by 5 rows.
Join squares to make two lengths of 24 Dogtooth squares each.
Join squares to make two lengths of 26 Dogtooth squares each.

Find the center seam of a 24 Dogtooth border and match to the center seam of the quilt top.
Pin outward to both ends and sew.
Repeat for bottom inner border.

Use 26 Dogtooth length for the side borders.
Attach them in the same way.
Attach the 12½" x 65½" outside borders to the quilt top and bottom first.
Attach the 12½" x 89½" side borders.

## Quilting Instructions

Draw quilting lines as desired.
Layer backing, batting, and top.
Baste and quilt.
Bind with straight grain strips brown fabric to equal 2¼" x 365" (nine 2¼" x 44" strips) binding.

*Four Blocks Continued...*

# Philadelphia Centennial Four-Block Eagle
## 79" x 79"

1776 – 1876 Philadelphia Centennial Eagle. Made in Pennsylvania, 1870 – 1876. The appliqués found here are taken directly from the quilt and are not symmetrical, adding to its stately charm.

# Philadelphia Centennial Four-Block Eagle

## Supplies

Basic sewing kit, page 6
Batting for 79" square
Backing for 79" square
Sewing machine for border piecing

## Fabric Requirements

7¼ yds. orange
1½ yds. green
1½ yds. red
¼ yd. yellow

30" Philadelphia Centennial Eagle Block

## Cutting Instructions (Patterns, page 87)

Instructions on the pattern pieces are for one block, unless otherwise noted.

Cut (4) orange 30½" blocks
Cut (2) orange 8½" x 63½" borders
Cut (2) orange 8½" x 79½" borders
Cut (8) 2¼" x 44" orange straight grain strips for binding
Cut (4) green A wing
Cut (4) green Ar wing
Cut (4) red B
Cut (4) yellow C
Cut (4) green D
Cut (4) red E
Cut (4) red F
Cut (4) red Fr
Cut (4) red G
Cut (1) red H
Cut (1) green I
Cut (1) orange fabric 26" square for Dogtooth squares
Cut (1) red fabric 26" square for Dogtooth squares
Cut out all appliqué pieces with a ⅛" seam allowance.

Four Blocks Continued...

## *Block Assembly*

Step 1: The eagles do not have to be symmetrically positioned. Fold a 30½" x 30½" block on the diagonal both ways and finger press. Position A and Ar in opposite corners. Position B so that it generally points to the center corner and so G will point towards the lower outer corner. Adjust accordingly so that C will cover the seam allowance on the lower head, wings, and tail.

Step 2: Needle turn under the wing edges. Appliqué the head, leaving beak and neck open. Iron the long side seam allowances on D. Pin it into the eagle's beak and appliqué E to the top of the baton.

Step 3: Position and pin F, Fr, and G in place. Turn under the seam allowances where they go under C. Appliqué the shield, then the feet and tail.

Step 4: Appliqué the remaining three blocks likewise (Fig. 1). Join two blocks together so that the eagles face the center. Repeat for other two blocks. Join the four blocks by matching the center seams and pinning outwards. Sew.

Step 5: Pin H over the center. Pin I over it. Appliqué the small star, then the large star.

Fig. 1

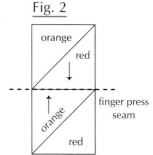

## *Inner Borders*

**Dogtooth Borders**

Using the requirements listed below, follow the instructions on page 7.

Make 164 Dogtooth squares.

Cut one 26" square from the red fabric.
Cut one 26" square from the orange fabric.
Draw a grid of 2⅜" squares, 10 rows by 9 rows.

Fig. 2

orange
red
↓
↑
orange
red
finger press seam

Using a ¼" seam, sew 20 Dogteeth together for the top inner border. Sew 20 again for the bottom inner border. Sew two borders of 22 Dogteeth for the side inner borders. Since the red tooth will be next ot the outer borders on all sides, make sure that you stitch them together as in Fig. 2.

Find the center of a 20 Dogtooth inner border and match it to the top center seam. Pin outwards. Sew. Repeat for bottom inner border.

Find the center of each 22 Dogtooth inner border. Match to center side seams pinning outwards. Sew.

## Outer Borders

Fold to find the center of the 8½" x 63½" top and bottom borders.
Match and pin from the center seam outwards. Sew.
Repeat for the 8½" x 79½" outside side borders.

## Finishing

Layer top, batting, and backing.
Quilt as desired.
Attach 2¼" x 325" (eight 2¼" x 44" strips) binding. Follow general directions, page 9.

*Four Blocks Continued...*

# Gordian Knot
### 76" x 76"

Cumberland County, PA, c. 1920. Also known as Mystic Maze.

# Gordian Knot

My best friend, Roslyn Dial, and I simplified this quilt design to a traditional machine pieced Log Cabin using the rotary strip technique. No need to cut hundreds of rectangles.

## Supplies

Basic sewing kit, page 6
Sewing machine
Batting for 76½" square
Backing for 76½" square

## Fabric Requirements

4 yds. white
2½ yds. blue

15" Gordian Knot block

## Cutting Instructions

Cut (2) white 8½" x 60½" borders
Cut (2) white 8½" x 76½" borders
Cut (16) white 2½" squares
Cut (4) white 4½" squares
Cut (4) 4½" x 7½" rectangles
Cut (2) white 4½" x 28½" rectangles
Cut (1) white 4½" x 60½" sashing

Cut out all borders, squares, and rectangles.

Cut 1½" wide strips from the remaining fabric. In general, a 90" wide fabric will yield about 24 blue 1½" wide strips and 10 white 1½" wide strips.

Fig. 1

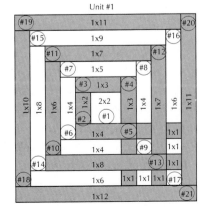

*Four Blocks Continued...*

# Gordian Knot

## Block Assembly

**Unit #1**

The circled numbers on the diagram indicate the order of attachment (Fig. 1).

Step 1:  Start with the white #1 2½" square. Sew a blue strip to it. Trim the threads. With the right sides together, trim the #2 blue strip even with the #1 white square.

Step 2:  Open to the right side. Finger press. Sew a blue strip in the #3 position. Trim even with the #2 edge.

Step 3:  Finger press open. Sew a blue strip in the #4 position. Trim even.

Step 4:  Finger press open. Sew a blue strip in the #5 position. Trim even.

Step 5:  Using the same method in steps 1–4, attach a white strip in the #6 & #7 positions.

Step 6:  Sew a 4½" white strip to a 1½" blue square. Attach the unit in the #8 position.

Step 7:  Sew a 1½" white square to a 1½" blue square then a 4½" white strip. Sew the unit in the #9 position.

Step 8:  Sew a blue strip into the #10, #11, #12, and the #13 positions.

Step 9:  Sew a white strip in the #14 and #15 positions,

Step 10: For position #16, assemble a 6½" white strip, 1½" blue square, 1½" white square, and then another 1½" blue square. Sew into place.

Step 11: For position #17, assemble the squares, white, blue, white, then blue, then a 6½" white strip. Sew into place.

Step 12: Sew blue strips into the #18, #19, #20, and #21 positions.

Repeat steps to make four #1 units.

**Unit #2 = 4" x 7" white rectangle**

**Unit #3 = five-strip unit, finished strips are 1" x 4".**

Step 1:  Alternate blue and white 1½" x 4½" strips (Fig. 2).

Step 2:  Make four #2 units.

Step 3:  Sew a #2 unit to a white 4" x 7" rectangle.

Step 4:  Sew each remaining #2 unit to a 4" x 7" rectangle.

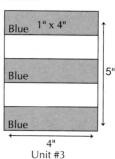

Fig. 2

Blue  1" x 4"

Blue

Blue

5"

4"
Unit #3

## Block Assembly

Step 1:  Sew Unit 2 to a 4½" x 7½" rectangle, Unit 3 (Fig. 3). Make four 2–3 units.

Step 2:  Sew a complete 2–3 unit to the side of Unit 1 (Fig. 3).

Step 3:  Sew another Unit 1 to the opposite side of the 2–3 unit.

Step 4:  Sew a 2–3 unit to the 4½" square to another 2–3 unit, forming a sash (Fig. 3).

Step 5:  Matching the vertical seams, pin to upper half of block and sew.

Step 6:  Make another Unit 1–2–3 unit — Unit 1 to form the bottom half of the block.

Step 7:  Join the bottom half to the sash, matching the vertical seams.

# Gordian Knot

## Joining the Blocks

Step 1: Sew two blocks to each vertical side of the 4½" x 28½" rectangle. Join the other two blocks in the same manner.

Step 2: Find the center of the 4½" x 60½" sashing. Finger press. Pin from the center working outward to the top two blocks. Sew. Pin and sew to bottom two blocks.

Step 3: Find the center of the 8½" x 60½" upper border. Match to the top center of the quilt top; pin working outward. Sew. Match the bottom border. Pin from the center outwards; sew.

Step 4: Find the center of each 8½" x 76½" side border. Match and pin from the center outward; sew.

## Dogtooth Binding

Step 1: Cut four 2" x 76½" strips.

Step 2: Mark dots on the strips (Fig. 4). Start by making a dot ½" in from both ends of the strip and 1¼" down from the top. Repeat dots every 1½". Mark offset dots on the raw edge with the first dot 1¼" in from the end of the strip. Repeat dots every 1½ ".

Step 3: Cut down 1¼" at the lower line dots.

Step 4: With right sides together, pin the binding to the back edge of the quilt top. Sew using a ¼" seam allowance.

Fig. 3 Full Block Pattern

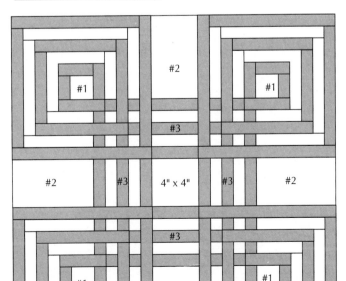

Four Blocks Continued...

Step 5: Fold up and over the quilt top. Needle turn under the vertical and horizontal raw edges of the ½" beginning indentation about ⅛" and appliqué.

Step 6: Fold under the right side of the first Dogtooth ⅛". Appliqué to the background within ¹⁄₁₆" of the marked dot. Take two stitches to anchor the point, then push the remaining raw edge towards the left side of the Dogtooth and under the anchored point. Continue to appliqué the left side of the Dogtooth. Take two stitches at the inner dot 1¼" down and proceed to next Dogtooth.

Step 7: Finish the end of the binding in the same way as the beginning. Repeat for remaining sides.

## Quilting Instructions

Mark the quilt. Layer the backing, batting, and top. Baste and quilt as desired.

Fig. 4

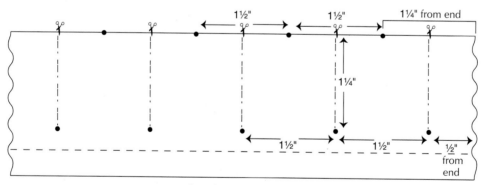

Marking the Dogtooth Binding

# Grape Wreaths
*88" x 88"*

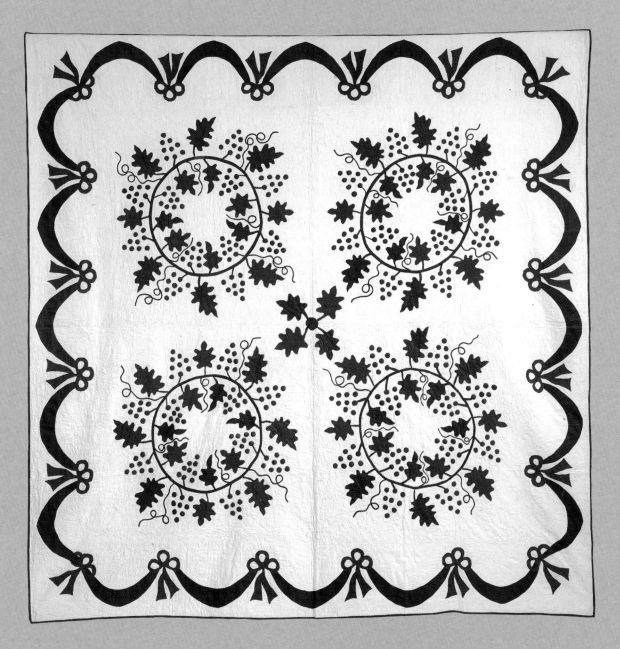

*CHwF, Baltimore, MD, 1871. Never washed, this battless summer quilt's stuffed grapes, randomly quilted vines, leaves, flowers, and borders have retained their pristine quality.*

# Grape Wreaths

## Supplies

Basic sewing kit, page 6
23" string
Batting for 88" square (optional)
Batting snippets
Backing for 88" square

## Fabric Requirements

6½ yds. white muslin
3 yds. red
3¾ yds. green

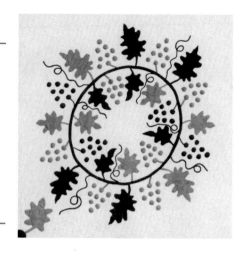

**34" Grape Wreath block**

## Cutting Instructions (Patterns, page 94)

Instructions on the pattern pieces are for one block, unless otherwise noted.

Cut (4) 34½" blocks of white background
Cut (4) 10½" x 90½" white borders
Cut 1¼" x 228" bias green for wreaths
Cut ¾" x 400" bias green for stems and tendrils
Cut ¾" x 75" bias red for stems
Cut (22) red A
Cut (18) green A
Cut (8) red B
Cut (16) green B
Cut (1) green C
Cut (20) green D
Cut (60) red E for borders
Cut (20) red F for borders
Cut (20) red G for borders
Cut (288) red grapes*
Cut (144) green grapes*

*Use a nickel as the grape template.

# Grape Wreaths

## Cutting Instructions

Step 1: Trace and cut all appliqué templates.

Step 2: Cut 1¼" bias green strips and join to make four 57" strips (228" total). These will be used for the grape wreaths. Fold each 1¼" x 57" section in half to form a ⅝" x 57" wide folded bias. Iron.

Step 3: Cut ¾" red bias strips. Join, fold, and iron to make ⅜" x 75" bias. Cut ¾" green bias strips. Join, fold and iron to make ⅜" x 400" bias. These bias strips will be used for the stems and tendrils.

## Block Assembly

Step 1: Fold a 34½" block in half horizontally and vertically. Finger press to mark center.

Step 2: Using the fold lines as a guide, mark 10" from the center on all four folds.

Step 3: Tie the string to a pencil. Measure out 20" and mark. This will serve as a compass. Pin the mark on the string to the center of the block. Holding the pencil perpendicular to the fabric, draw a 20" circle on the block. The circle should fall near the 10" marks on the folds. It is the guide to place the green bias.

Step 4: Pin the ⅝" x 57" green bias on the circle with the raw edges about ⅛" inside the circle (Fig. 1). Just outside the drawn circle, use a running stitch to anchor the bias tape. Continue around circle and overlap the beginning end by ¼".

Step 5: Mark ½" openings on the green bias circle where the leaves, tendrils, and stems will be placed. For placement see block on page 46.

Step 6: Fold the bias tape up and over the raw edge and appliqué down except for the marked openings.

Step 7: Place and pin three red A's and four green A's inside the wreath. Needle turn appliqué.

Step 8: Using the technique explained in Step 4, place, pin, and appliqué four green tendrils, two red stems, and two green stems cut from the ⅜" wide bias.

Step 9: Pin each 9-grape bunch in place above a matching color stem. Insert a bit of batting before appliquéing down.

Repeat steps 1–9 for remaining three blocks.

Fig. 1

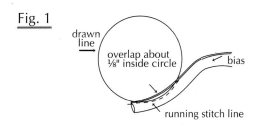

drawn line

overlap about ⅛" inside circle

bias

running stitch line

Four Blocks Continued...

## Joining the Blocks

Sew two blocks together using a ¼" seam. Sew the other two blocks together likewise. Match and pin at the center seam of each pair. Pin together working outward. Sew.

Place and pin C on the center of the quilt top. Equally space and pin two red A's and two green A's. Appliqué the leaves, then the circle.

## Borders

Spread the finished quilt top out and smooth away any wrinkles. Place the four borders with the ends overlapping. Pin a temporary miter so that the swag and bow appliqués may be properly positioned.

There are five swags for each border. Starting with the center swag, pin into position. Working outwards, add the remaining bows and swags. The bow pieces, E, F, and G, should be placed as shown in Fig. 2.

Center the bow on the mitered corners. The swag on either side will have their ends tucked under the side of the bow.

Baste the pieces leaving the last few inches of the swags that touch the corner bows unbasted.

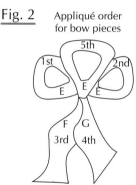

Fig. 2    Appliqué order for bow pieces

The corner bows and swag ends will be appliquéd after the borders are attached. Appliqué the other swags and bows. For the bows, appliqué in the order indicated in Fig. 2.

Miter the borders and attach to quilt top. Finish appliquéing the corner swags. Reposition the corner bows and appliqué (Fig. 3).

Fig. 3

## Finishing

Layer backing, batting (optional), and top. Baste together. Quilt as desired. Make 2¼" x 360" (nine 2¼" x 44" strips) red binding. Attach following general directions, page 9.

# The Vintage Oak Is the Wine of Life

## 72" x 72"

The original Scherenschnitte pattern was designed for my mother as a Mother's Day gift, May 12, 1996. The standing oak of my life, I hope, as one of her little acorns, that her wisdom flows through me as well.

# The Vintage Oak Is the Wine of Life

## Supplies

Basic sewing kit, page 6
Thread to match oak leaf and acorn appliqués
Background block thread
Batting for 72" square
Backing for 72" square
Poster or tagboard

36" Vintage Oak Is the Vine of Life block

## Fabric Requirements

4½ yds. for block background and binding
4¼ yds. for Scherenschnitte oak leaf and acorn design on each block

## Cutting Instructions (Patterns, page 96)

Cut (4) 36½ blocks for background
Cut (4) 36½ blocks for Scherenschnitte oak leaf and acorn design
Cut 2¼" wide straight grain strips to equal 295" long binding (seven 2¼" x 44" strips)

## Template Assembly

Trace and cut out the oak leaf and acorn pattern pieces. Tape together as indicated. Transfer to poster or tagboard. Trace and cut out. Label the front and back as per Fig. 1.

Fig. 1

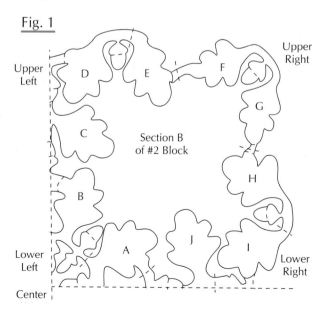

Upper Left

Upper Right

D  E  F

G

C  Section B of #2 Block

H

B

A  J  I

Lower Left

Lower Right

Center

## Tracing Instructions

Read through the instructions before beginning. The pattern will be flipped four times. The pattern design is rotated for each block so the full layout will not be apparent until it is put together. After tracing a block, set the template aside in the exact position it was traced. The step by step instructions are based on the template being in the preceding step's position.

Step 1: Number each 36½" x 36½" block 1 through 4.

Step 2: Fold each of the 36½" blocks into quarters and iron the folds lightly to make guidelines. Mark the four sections of the #2 block (Fig. 2).

Step 3: Place the template over section B with the Upper Right corner of the template in the upper right-hand corner of the section. Trace.

Step 4: Flip the pattern top over bottom onto section C. The template corner labeled Lower Right should now be in the upper right hand corner of this section. Trace.

Step 5: Flip the pattern right over left onto section D. The template should now be face up with the corner labeled Lower Left in the upper right hand corner. Trace.

Step 6: Flip the pattern bottom over top onto section A. The Upper Left labeled corner should now be in the upper right hand corner. Trace.

Step 7: Do not cut out the template.

Step 8: Repeat tracing instructions 2 – 8 for the remaining sections of the blocks.

Step 9: Trace the acorn from the block's center in one corner of each block to form the center of the quilt.

Step 10: Trace the block design on the oak leaf and acorn fabric. Once each block has been traced, baste the entire block to its background block.

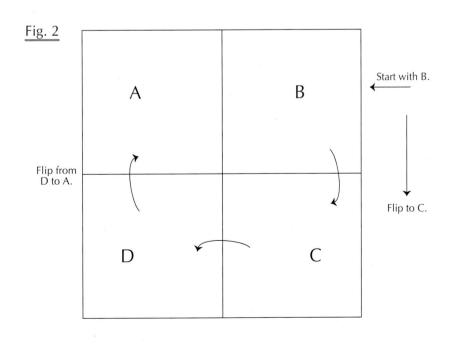

Fig. 2

*Four Blocks Continued...*

# The Vintage Oak Is the Wine of Life

## Appliqué Instructions

Carefully cut away ⅛" from all drawn lines except those along the center seam edges. Leave a ¼" seam allowance on these center edges. They will be caught with the joining of the four blocks. It is best to cut about 5" at a time, and needle turn appliqué section by section. Do not appliqué along the center seam edges.

## Joining the Blocks

Joined correctly, a circle of acorns should be formed in the center of the quilt. First, join blocks #1 and #2. Match, pin, and sew. Join blocks #3 and #4 likewise. Match and pin the center seam of the top two blocks with the lower blocks' center seam. Pin from the center outwards. Sew (Fig. 3).

## Finishing Instructions

Draw quilting lines as desired. Layer backing, batting, and top. Baste together. Quilt. Apply binding, following general instructions, page 9.

Fig. 3

Block #1          Block #2

Block #3          Block #4

# North, East, South & West, My Captain Is the Best

## 76" x 81"

This quilt was made by the author for her husband, John, who loves sailing. But after three sailboats, Linda was still a landlubber and so John opted for the tandem (symbolized in the center appliqué) he now captains. 1996.

# North, East, South & West, My Captain Is the Best

The main pattern in this quilt, designed for machine piecing, is a 24" Mariner's Compass. It was my first attempt at machine piecing. The novice to advanced machine piecing quilter can produce a wonderful Mariner's Compass quilt by making four 42" blocks with wave borders.

A personal touch may be affected by adding an original center appliqué. The template may be free handed, cut from coloring books, or by tracing a projected picture on a wall. Just transfer the tracings onto template plastic and cut out.

The pattern includes instructions for a 4, 8, 16, or 32 point compass per block. The same compass may be used for each block, alternated, or one of each. The compasses all fit together in the same way with the larger pieces breaking down into smaller pieced units as more points are added. If the same fabric is used in more than one compass, the fabric yardages will need to be increased accordingly.

42" blocks in
North, East, South & West,
My Captain Is the Best

## Supplies

Basic sewing kit, page 6
Batting for 84½" square
Backing for 84½" square

## Fabric Requirements

5 yds. background material
5 yds. for waves
2¼" x 338" binding (extra yardage from background waves can be used)

| | |
|---|---|
| ⅛ yd. for Template A | ¼ yd. for Template F |
| ¼ yd. for Template B | ¼ yd. for Template G |
| ¼ yd. for Template C | ½ yd. for Template H |
| ¼ yd. for Template D | ¼ yd. for Template I |
| ¼ yd. for Template E | ¼ yd. for Template J |

*Template yardages given assuming no fabric will be repeated in another compass.

## Cutting Instructions (Patterns, page 106)

Make plastic templates and trace around them on the wrong side of the fabric, except for the wave templates that are to be appliquéd to the 42½" compasses. Mark the sewing line by marking a dot on the fabric inside the template holes. See general guidelines, page 6.

Cut (4) 42½" blocks from background fabric
Cut (4) 42½" blocks from wave fabric

| 4 Pt Compass | 8 Pt Compass | 16 Pt Compass | 32 Pt Compass |
|---|---|---|---|
| Cut (8) A pieces | Cut (8) A pieces | Cut (8) A pieces | Cut (8) A pieces |
| Cut (4) B pieces | Cut (8) B pieces | Cut (8) B pieces | Cut (8) B pieces |
| Cut (32) F pieces | Cut (32) F pieces | Cut (8) E pieces | Cut (32) C pieces |
| Cut (32) G pieces | Cut (32) G pieces | Cut (32) F pieces | Cut (16) D pieces |
| *Cut (4) J + Jr pieces | Cut (8) H pieces | Cut (32) G pieces | Cut (8) E pieces |
| | | Cut (16) I pieces | Cut (32) F pieces |
| | | | Cut (32) G pieces |

*Trace J on paper, flip on fold line and trace Jr to make complete template. Trace on template plastic.

**Hint:** Cut fabrics for one compass at a time. Keeping track of 500 pieces divided between four different blocks can be unnecessarily intimidating.

**Reminder:** Seam allowances are already added to the templates. The dots, cut and marked as explained in the general guidelines, page 6, are the machine starting and stopping points.

## Block Assembly — 4 Point Mariner's Compass

Instructions are for one compass.

Step 1: Sew two A's by matching the dots on two long sides. Sew dot to dot (Fig. 1).
Repeat with three more pairs of A's. Join two A pairs (Fig. 2). Repeat with remaining two units. Pin and sew halves making sure center points match (Fig. 3).

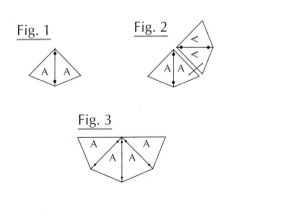

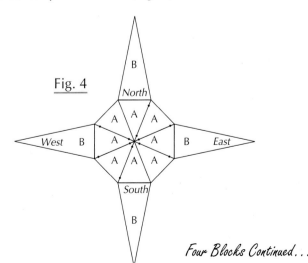

*Four Blocks Continued...*

Step 2: Sew four B's to the base of the north, east, south, and west A triangles (Fig. 4).

Step 3: Sew 32 F's to 32 G's (Fig. 5). Leave last G unsewn to first F. F–G band will curve to form a circle. Set aside.

Step 4: Sew base of J unit to base of northeast triangle A. Pin and sew from dot A to dot C. Pin and sew from dot A to dot B (Fig. 6).

Step 5: Repeat step 4 for remaining J units.

Step 6: Pick up string of joined F's and G's (Step 3). Starting with the north B tip, match dots and pin the last G, right sides together, to the left side tip of north B tip (Fig. 7). Match dots of eight G's between north B tip and west B tip around the edge of the northwest J unit. Continue around the remaining J unit sections. With right sides together, sew down.

Fig. 5

Fig. 6

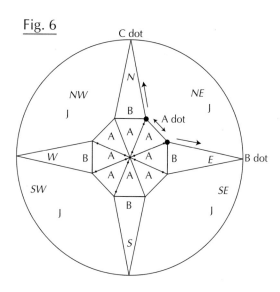

Fig. 7

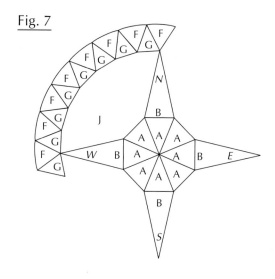

## Block Assembly — 8 Point Mariner's Compass

Step 1: Sew eight A's together as in Step 1, 4 Point. Compass instructions (Figs. 1–3).

Fig. 8

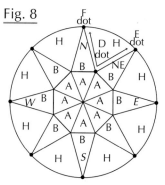

Step 2: Sew the base of each B to the base of each A (Fig. 8).

Step 3: Sew 32 F's and 32 G's together to create a curved band (Fig. 5).

Step 4: Pin and sew H from dot D to dot E (Fig. 8). Pin and sew from dot D to dot F.

Step 5: Repeat procedure for remaining H's.

Step 6: Attach F–G band beginning with the north B tip, working counterclockwise, matching the dots to the H's edges (Fig. 7).

# North, East, South & West, My Captain Is the Best

## Block Assembly — 16 Point Mariner's Compass

Step 1: Sew eight A's together as in step 1 of the 4 Point Compass instructions (Figs. 1–3).

Step 2: Sew the base of each B to the base of each A (Fig. 8).

Step 3: Sew 32 F's to 32 G's creating a circular band (Fig. 5).

Step 4: Sew an I to each side of an E. Repeat, making eight units (Fig. 9).

Step 5: Pin and sew from dot D to dot E uniting one I–E–I unit to a B (Fig. 10). Pin and sew from dot D to dot F uniting the remaining side to opposite B.

Step 6: Attach F–G band beginning with the north B tip, working counter-clockwise, matching the dots to the H edges (Fig. 7).

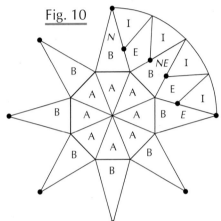

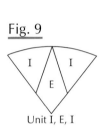

Fig. 9

Unit I, E, I

## Block Assembly — 32 Point Mariner's Compass

Step 1: Sew eight A's together as per Step 1 in the 4 Pt. Compass instructions (Fig. 1–3).

Step 2: Sew the base of each B to the base of each A (Fig. 8).

Step 3: Sew 32 F's to 32 G's creating a circular band (Fig. 5).

Step 4: With right sides together and matching dots, sew C to each side of D (Fig. 11).

Step 5: Sew a C–D–C unit to each side of E, the C–D–C unit replacing I used in Step 4 of the 16 Point Compass. Match dots, pin, and sew this new unit from Dot D to Dot E then Dot D to Dot F (Fig. 10).

Step 6: Attach F–G band beginning with the north B tip, working counter-clockwise, matching the dots to the H edges (Fig. 8).

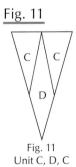

Fig. 11

Fig. 11
Unit C, D, C

## Appliquéing to Background Block

Iron block so that center lies flat. There should be no ripples in the compass. Fold background block in half vertically and horizontally to find center. Finger press. Center compass over the block and pin. Needle turn the edges of compass and appliqué in place.

*Four Blocks Continued...*

## Wave Border

Join the wave pattern sections and trace ¼ of the wave section onto the right side of the 42½" block of wave fabric starting at the lower left corner. The template should extend from the left side center around to the bottom center. Flip pattern over to trace the lower right corner. Continue flipping and tracing on around the block. Cut out about ⅛" away from lines. This is the seam allowance for needle turn appliquéing. Place and pin onto the Mariner's Compass block. Appliqué in place. Repeat for other three blocks.

## Joining the Blocks

Sew two finished blocks together. Repeat with remaining two blocks. Sew the four blocks together first matching and pinning the center seams.

## Center Appliqué

The center appliqué is optional, but an anchor, ship's wheel, crossed oars, or a canoe can continue the nautical theme. Fold an 8½" x 11" or larger piece of paper in half and draw half of the object on the fold. Cut out. Unfold and trace onto template plastic. Transfer to right side of fabric. Place on quilt and needle turn appliqué.

## Binding

Make 2¼" x 330" (eight 2¼" x 44" strips) binding. General directions, page 9.

## Quilting

Layer backing, batting, and top. Baste. Quilt as desired or draw random squiggly lines across background fabric to indicate waves. Echo quilt on and around the waves themselves. On the compasses, quilt down the center of the points. Use S-type squigglies on pieces F and G. Outline quilt any center appliqué.

# Whig-Harrison Rose
### 90" x 90"

Traditional colors of red, gold, and green are used in the flowers of this Whig-Harrison Rose quilt. The rose centers are bordered with rosebuds in an asymmetrical design. Made by the author, 1994.

# Whig-Harrison Rose

## Supplies

Basic sewing kit, page 6
Batting for 90" square
Backing for 90" square
1 large sheet template plastic

## Fabric Requirements

4 yds. background color
½ yd. yellow
½ yd. red
1 yd. dark red
2 yds. dark green
½ yd. medium green print
3½ yds. border and binding fabric
5" square for center appliqué center
6" square for center appliqué middle petals
8" square for center appliqué outer petals

35" Whig Harrison Rose block

## Cutting Instructions *(Patterns, page 117)*

Instructions on the pattern pieces are for one block, unless otherwise noted.

Cut (4) 35½" blocks of background fabric
Cut (2) 10½" x 70½" top and bottom borders of print
Cut (2) 10½" x 90½" side borders of print
Cut & make 2¼" x 365" (nine 2¼" x 44" strips) binding
Cut (4) red A
Cut (36) dark red B
Cut (36) yellow C
Cut (16) green print D
Cut (16) dark green E

Cut (16) red F
Cut (16) dark red G
Cut (8) yellow H
Cut (8) yellow Hr
Cut (56) red H
Cut (40) red Hr
Cut (48) dark green I
Cut (48) dark green Ir
Cut (1) each of J, K, and L

Trace all templates on right side of fabric, *except* B. Trace B on wrong side of red since the short straight sides will be pieced. Add a ⅛" seam allowance on all pieces.

# Whig-Harrison Rose

## Block Assembly

Step 1: Piece short straight sides of B's together to form a circle. Finger press under curved edges on pencil lines.

Step 2: Fold background block in half twice to find center. Finger press center and open.

Step 3: Position circle of B's in center and pin. Lay A over raw edges of B's inner circle. Needle turn under A's edges and appliqué.

Step 4: Finger press outer curved edge of C's on pencil line. Insert C's between B's and temporarily pin in place.

Step 5: Insert and position six-pointed leaves under Harrison Rose. Pin. Insert, position, and pin four E rose branches under Harrison Rose.

Step 6: Appliqué B's over C's, leaves, and rose branches.

Step 7: Appliqué C's down over leaves and rose branches.

Step 8: Finish sewing down leaves and branches, inserting four H buds where necessary.

Step 9: Position and appliqué red F's to G's. Position each F – G at the top ends of the rose branches and appliqué down.

Step 10: Option: number of bud stems can vary.

Step 11: Surround the Whig-Harrison Rose with a circle of buds. Trace the bud stem from the E rose branch onto top of dark green fabric. Using red, pink, and yellow, make buds using Template H on the right side of the fabrics. Only trace four yellow buds, which should be placed under the bud stems pointing towards the center Harrison Rose.

Step 12: Lay the bud stems around the floral "X" with the stems under the buds. Adjust so design is pleasing to the eye, and pin. Insert the buds, alternating the red and pink, and appliqué all pieces in place.

Join the four blocks.

## Center Appliqué

Step 1: Trace each pattern (J, K, L) individually onto template plastic. Trace onto right side of fabric.

Step 2: Position J on K. Pin and needle turn the seam allowance and appliqué.

Step 3: Pin the J–K unit on L and appliqué.

Step 4: Center the J–K–L unit over the center and appliqué.

## Borders

Fold and finger press the center of the 10½" x 70½" borders.

Match the top border and pin outwards from the center seam. Sew.

*Four Blocks Continued...*

Repeat for the bottom border.

Find the center of the 10½" x 90½" side borders.
Match and pin each from the center seam outwards. Sew.

## Quilting Instructions

Mark the four blocks first with the fan quilting motif. Cover the entire quilt except for the center motif. Leave a ¼" margin around the center motif. Mark the center motif with the shown quilting lines (Fig. 1).

Layer backing, batting, and top. Baste, then quilt.

Apply binding following general directions, page 9.

Fig. 1

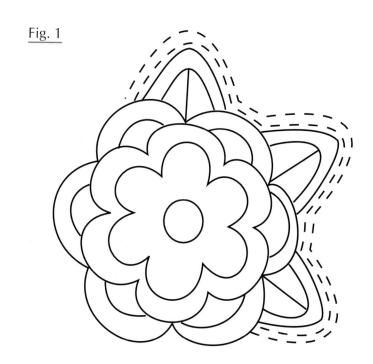

# Mary Ann Smith's Quilt
## 66" x 66"

According to Martha Olive Smith Dulaney, her mother, Mary Ann Matheny Smith was a cousin to Mark Twain, though the exact family link to Clemens family is not clear. Made in Tennessee, 1860. Mrs. Emogene (Neal) Shepard, granddaughter of Martha Olive Smith Dulaney, can remember her grandmother retelling how Mary Ann would talk about the Clemens and the Mathenys.

# Mary Ann Smith's Quilt

Mary Ann Matheny Smith was the great-grandmother of Emogene Shepard who selected me as the next caretaker of her quilt. To make a modern-day version of this quilt, one might use a beige print for the background, plaid for the inner border, with red, green, and white for the vase of flowers.

## Supplies

Basic sewing kit, page 6
Paper
Batting for 66" square
Backing for 66" square

20" Vase of Flowers block
from Mary Ann Smith's quilt

## Fabric Requirements

3¾ yds. white for blocks and outside borders
2 yds. green
1¼ yds. gold
1¼ yds. red (the red in the quilt has faded to brown)

## Cutting Instructions (Patterns, page 122)

Instructions on the pattern pieces are for one block, unless otherwise noted.

Cut (4) 20½" white print blocks
Cut (2) 10½" x 46½" white outside borders
Cut (4) 3½" x 40½" inner red borders
Cut (2) 10½" x 66½" white outside borders
Cut 2¼" x 270" (seven 2¼" x 44" strips) white binding
Cut (4) 3½" gold squares

| Red | Gold | Green |
|---|---|---|
| Cut (4) A | Cut (4) B | Cut (4) C |
| Cut (2) E | Cut (4) D | Cut (8) G |
| Cut (2) Er | Cut (8) H | Cut (48) I |
| Cut (8) F | Cut (8) J | Cut (8) M |
| Cut (4) K w/o circle | Cut (4) K | Cut (6) P |
| Cut (4) L | Cut (8) N | Cut (4) R |
| Cut (2) P | Cut (2) O | |
| | Cut (4) P | |

*Four Blocks Continued...*

Cut (14) Q any combination of gold, red, or green
Cut (8) Q with stems lengthened 1½" — any combination of gold, red, or green
Cut (306) S any combination of red, gold, and green

Trace A, B, C, and D on the *wrong* side of the fabric. Trace all other templates on the right side of the fabric. Remember to leave a ⅛" seam allowance.

Cut out appliqué pieces and sort for each block and border. Set aside in individual envelopes or plastic bags.

Cut and make 2" x 260" of green bias for the serpentine border vines
Cut and make 1" x 300" of green bias for chalice flower and berry stems
Cut and make ⅜" x 60" of gold, red, or green bias for border berry and leaf stems

## Block Assembly

Step 1: Assemble pieces A, B, C, and D (Fig. 1). Place the unit about 2" up from the bottom center of the 20½" square block. Position E (on two blocks it will be the same and reversed on the others) with the edges tucked under the chalice. Appliqué the chalice, except the upper rim (D), in place. Appliqué K into piece (Fig. 1).

Step 2: Fold wrong sides together, and press the 1" x 300" green bias. Cut seven 11" to 15" lengths for chalice flower and berry stems. Cut two 6" to 8" lengths for short center stems. Mark a pattern line, Fig. 2, and pin the raw edges a length to it placing the raw edges ⅛" over the line. Sew a running stitch just under the pattern line to anchor the folded bias. Turn the bias up and appliqué down the folded side about 2"–3" out from the chalice. Repeat for each stem.

Fig. 1

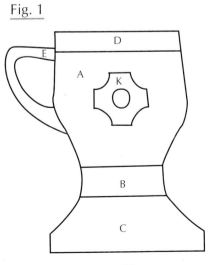

*Four Blocks Continued...*

Fig. 2

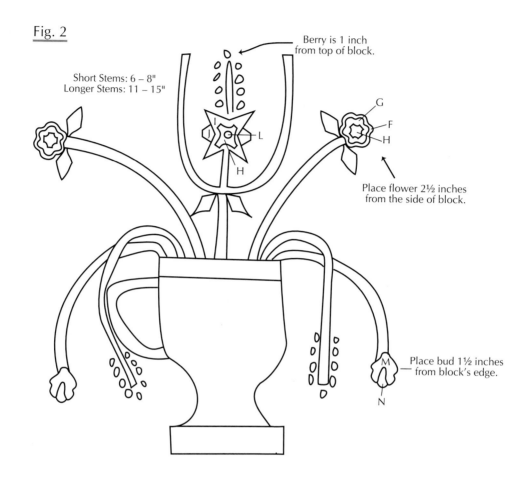

Berry is 1 inch from top of block.

Short Stems: 6 – 8"
Longer Stems: 11 – 15"

G
F
H

Place flower 2½ inches from the side of block.

Place bud 1½ inches from block's edge.

M
N

Step 3: Appliqué D down over the appliquéd stems. Finish appliquéing the stems *omitting* the center stem area above and below the center flower.

Step 4: For the center flower, pin four I leaves in place. Insert two J sepals (Fig. 2). Appliqué the J's first, then the I's. Finish appliquéing the center stem straight over the leaves. Appliqué the L onto the white K. Center the K–L unit over the leaves and appliqué.

Step 5: Appliqué H onto a G. Appliqué H–G to F. Place the F–G–H unit on the correct stem and appliqué (Fig. 2).

Step 6: Position M calyx on the stem. Insert N bud. Appliqué the calyx over the bud, then finish the flower.

Step 7: Place and appliqué the berries (S). There are nine berries to each cluster (Fig. 2). The berries can be stuffed with a bit of batting before appliquéing the edges.

Repeat for each block.

# Mary Ann Smith's Quilt

## Joining the Blocks

Join the upper two blocks, then the lower two blocks.
Matching the center seams and pinning outwards, join the two pieces. Sew.

## Inside Borders

Sew two 3½" x 40½" red borders to the quilt top and bottom.
Sew four 3½" x 3½" gold squares to the ends of the remaining two borders (see quilt photo).
Sew the side borders to the quilt.

## Outside Borders

Fold the 10½" x 46½" borders in half lengthwise (at 23"), then again (at 11½").
Lightly press the folds. These will serve as guidelines for the serpentine bias vine appliqué.

Trace and tape the guideline, page 99, together on two 12" x 10½" pieces of paper. The curve should be 11½" long.

Trace the curve onto each 23" section starting at the right edge of the border 5" down from the top edge on the right side of the fabric. Notice that the beginning 11½" of the line is on the top half of the border and on the bottom half of the last 11½" of the border. Repeat tracing for other 46½" border.

On the 10½" x 66½" borders, mark 10" inward from the ends of the borders and pin (Fig. 3). Draw vine guidelines up to these pin marks. Start marking the vine guidelines 5" from the top right end pin. Mark as before, but end at the left end pin. Repeat process for the remaining 66½" border.

Lay the drawn bottom border face up. Place the side borders perpendicular to it. Trace the corner guidelines in the 10" corner of the side border. Repeat for the other three corners.

Using a running stitch, attach the 2" green bias (now folded and pressed to 1" wide) with the raw edges ⅛" overlapping the line. Place and pin the ⅜" bias (folded to 3⁄16") stems under the vine (Fig. 4). Turn under the seam allowances before appliquéing the 1" serpentine vine over the stem edges. Finish appliquéing the 1" bias, then the 3⁄16" stems.

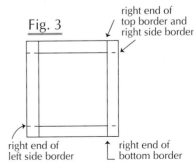

Fig. 3

right end of
top border and
right side border

right end of
left side border

right end of
bottom border

*Four Blocks Continued...*

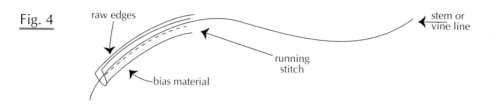

Fig. 4

raw edges

stem or vine line

running stitch

bias material

Place and pin all P, Q, and R leaves.
Appliqué the leaves and stuff the berries with a bit of batting before appliquéing.

Position the O's over the top and bottom center seams about 2½" from the edge and over-lapping the vine (Fig. 5).

Insert three long-stemmed Q's in the flower pots. Pin in place.
Appliqué.

## Quilting Instructions

Trace quilting lines as desired. Mary Ann quilted ¼" random lines all over the quilt with scattered leaves following the template lines.

Layer the backing, batting, and top. Baste, then quilt.
Make and attach 2¼" x 270" (seven 2¼" x 44" strips) binding as indicated in the general directions, page 9.

Fig. 5

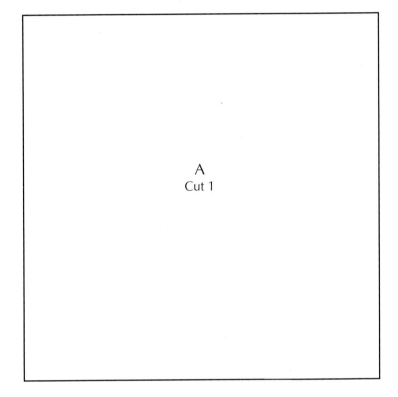

A
Cut 1

D
Cut 4

C & Cr

8 & 8r Green
8 & 8r Pink

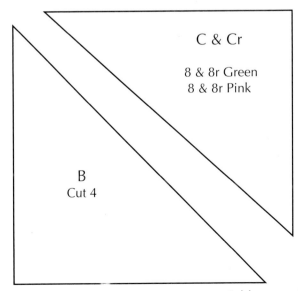

B
Cut 4

Add seam allowances.

*Four Blocks Continued...*

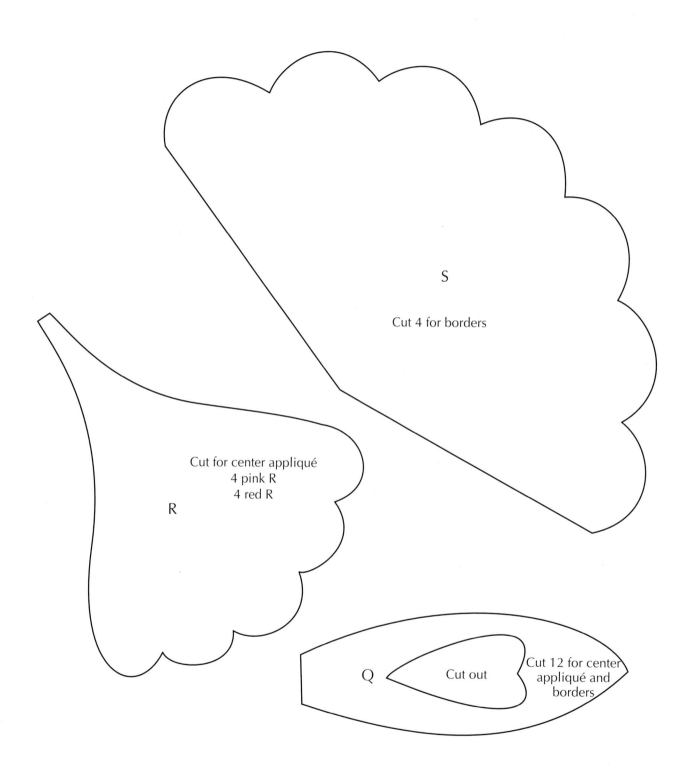

S

Cut 4 for borders

Cut for center appliqué
4 pink R
4 red R

R

Q        Cut out        Cut 12 for center
appliqué and
borders

Add seam allowances.

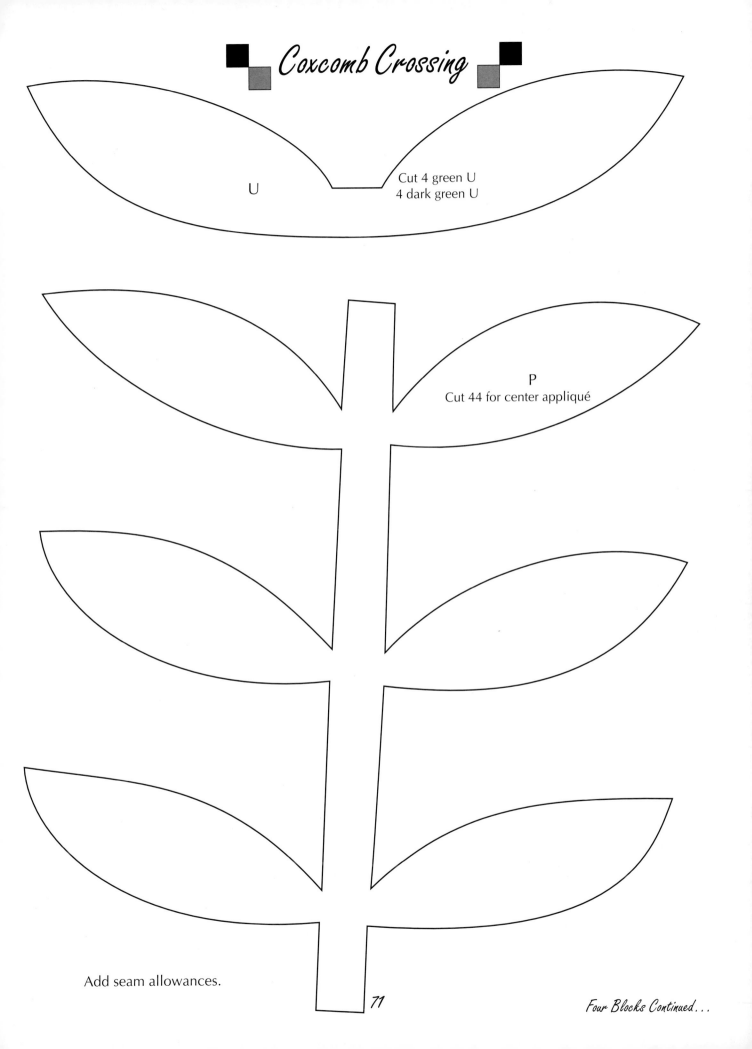

U

Cut 4 green U
4 dark green U

P
Cut 44 for center appliqué

Add seam allowances.

*Four Blocks Continued…*

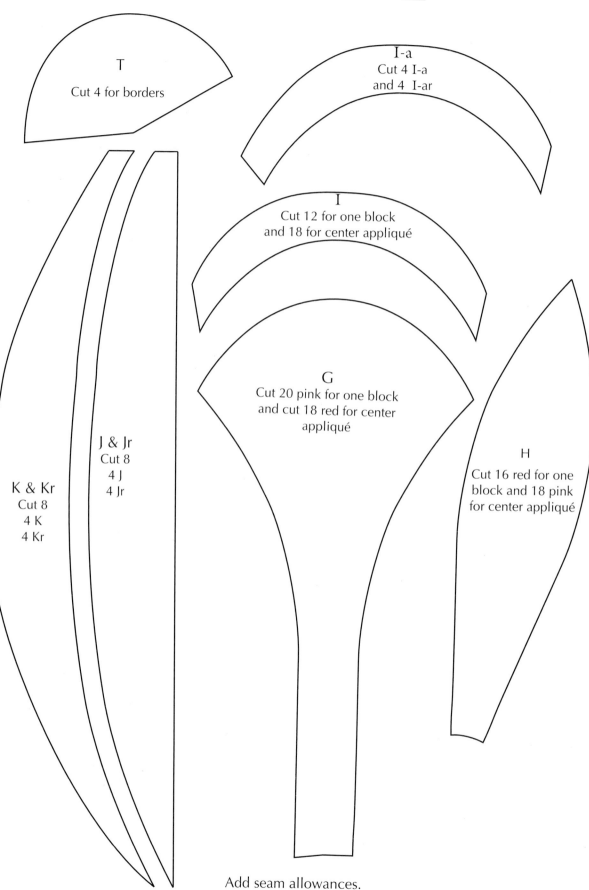

T

Cut 4 for borders

I-a
Cut 4 I-a
and 4  I-ar

I
Cut 12 for one block
and 18 for center appliqué

G
Cut 20 pink for one block
and cut 18 red for center
appliqué

J & Jr
Cut 8
4 J
4 Jr

K & Kr
Cut 8
4 K
4 Kr

H
Cut 16 red for one
block and 18 pink
for center appliqué

Add seam allowances.

Four Blocks Continued...

O
Cut 4
White

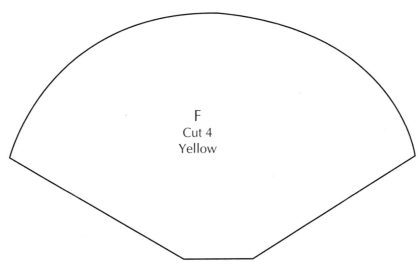

F
Cut 4
Yellow

Add seam allowances.

*Four Blocks Continued...*

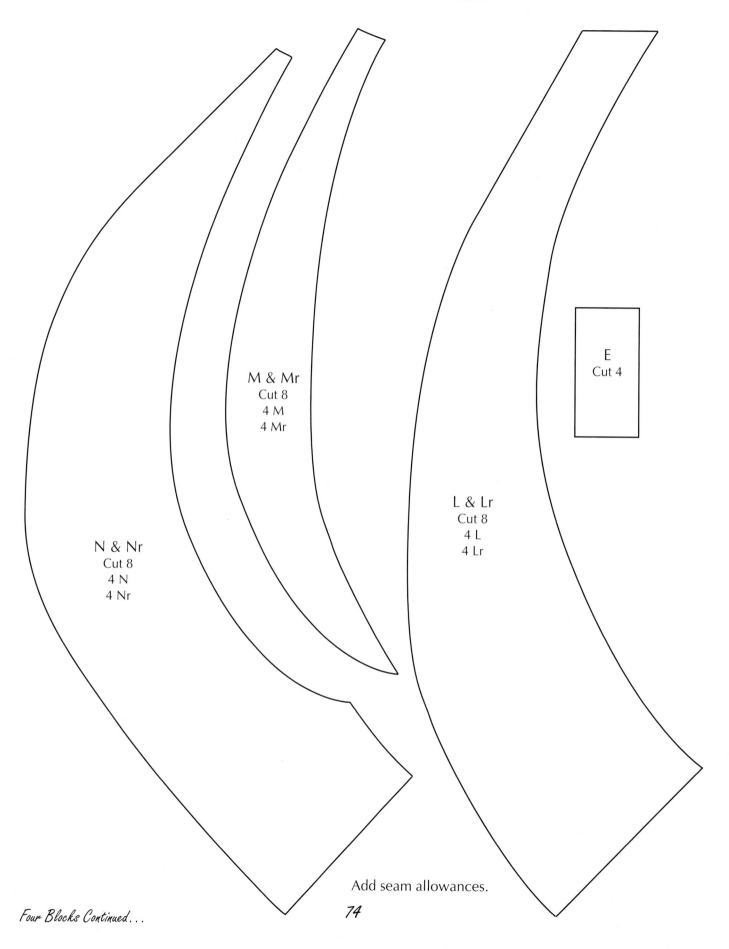

M & Mr
Cut 8
4 M
4 Mr

E
Cut 4

N & Nr
Cut 8
4 N
4 Nr

L & Lr
Cut 8
4 L
4 Lr

Add seam allowances.

# Oak Leaf & Reel with Tulips

A

Cut 1 for each block

Pattern
Guide

Add seam allowances.

*Four Blocks Continued...*

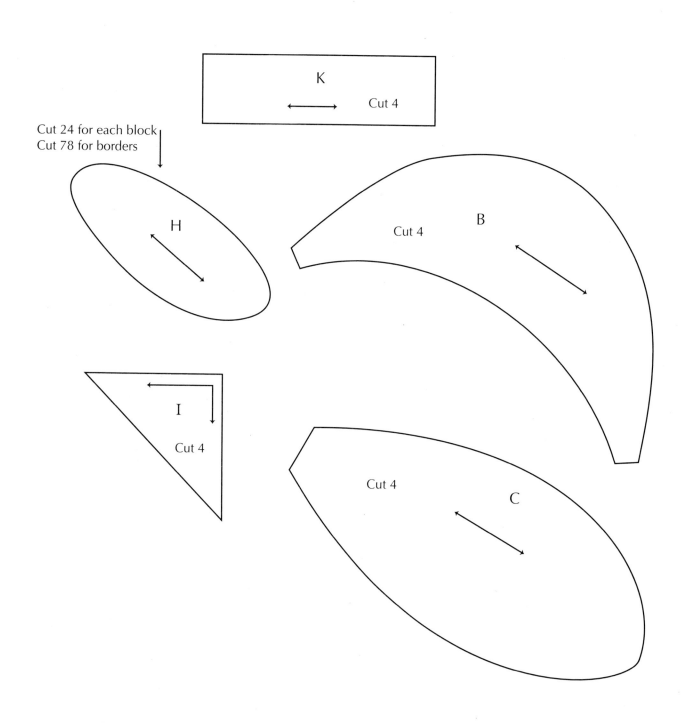

K
Cut 4

Cut 24 for each block
Cut 78 for borders

H

B
Cut 4

I
Cut 4

Cut 4
C

Add seam allowances.

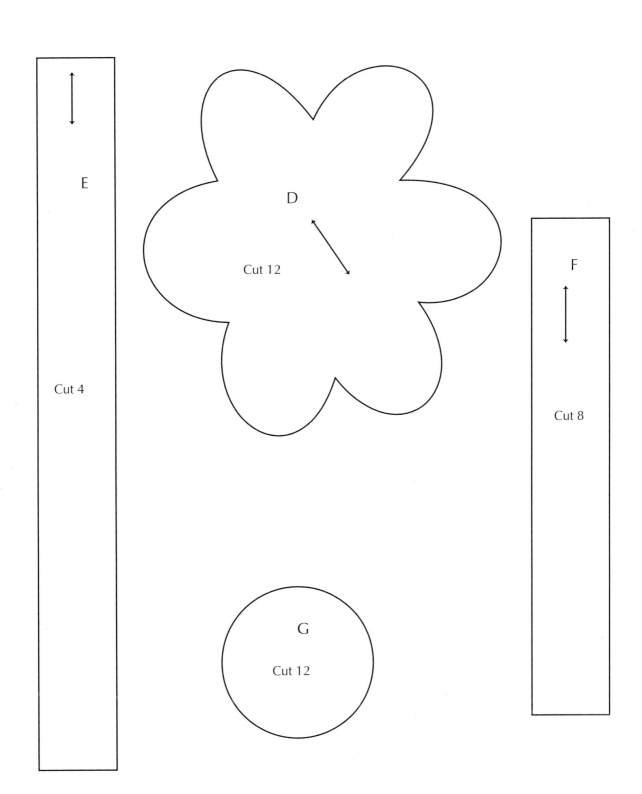

E

Cut 4

D

Cut 12

F

Cut 8

G

Cut 12

Add seam allowances.

*Four Blocks Continued...*

L & Lr

For sashing, cut 4 red L and 4 red Lr
6 pumpkin L and 6 pumpkin Lr

O

Cut 26 for borders

J

Cut 4

Add seam allowances.

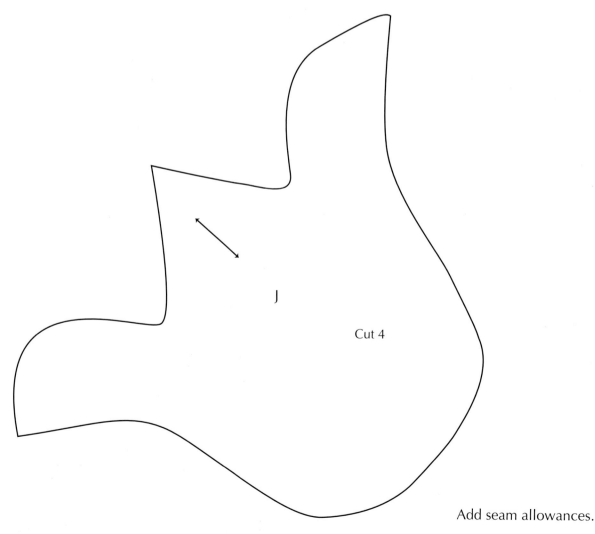

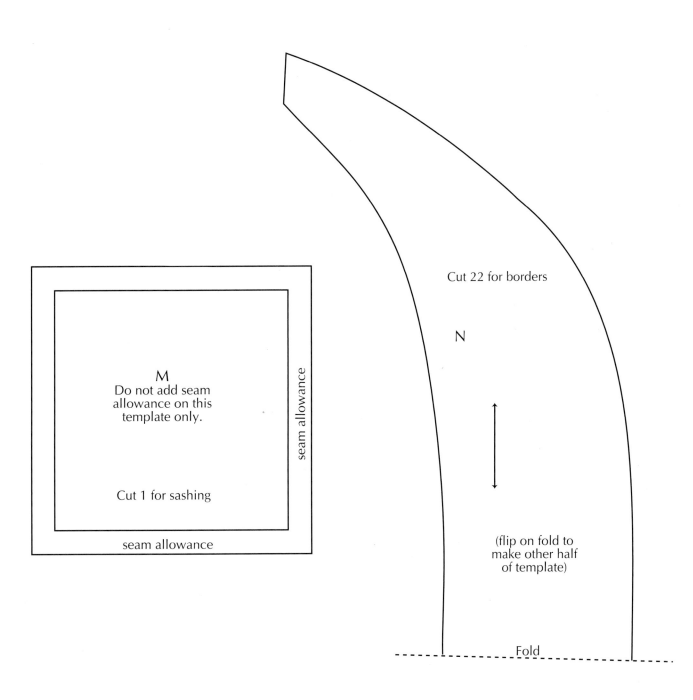

M
Do not add seam
allowance on this
template only.

Cut 1 for sashing

seam allowance

seam allowance

Cut 22 for borders

N

(flip on fold to
make other half
of template)

Fold

Add seam allowances to appliqué pieces.

*Four Blocks Continued . . .*

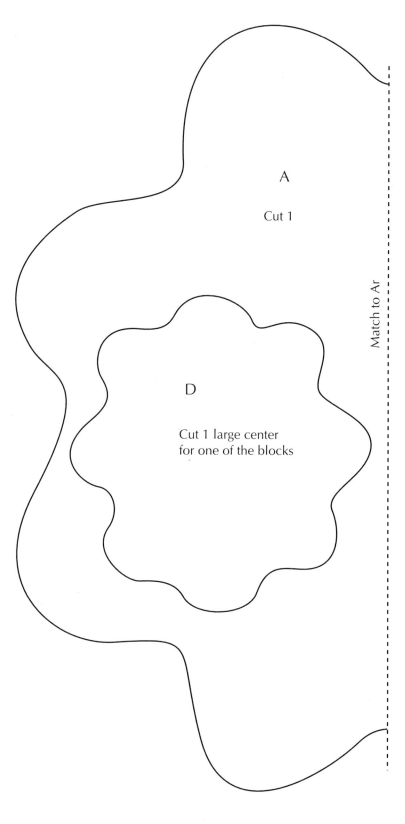

A

Cut 1

Match to Ar

D

Cut 1 large center
for one of the blocks

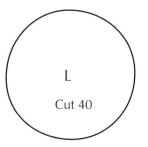

L

Cut 40

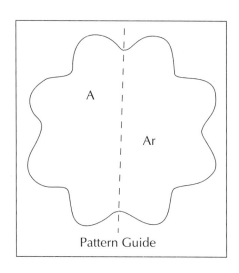

A

Ar

Pattern Guide

Add seam allowances.

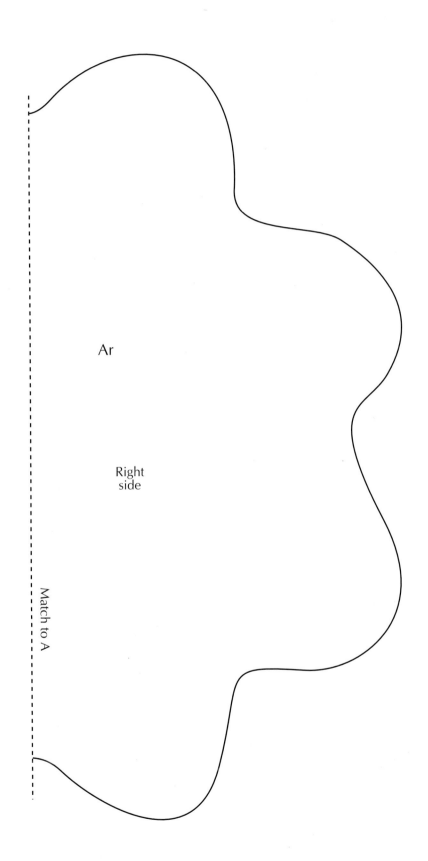

Ar

Right
side

Match to A

Add seam allowances.

*Four Blocks Continued...*

# Amish Rose of Sharon Wreath

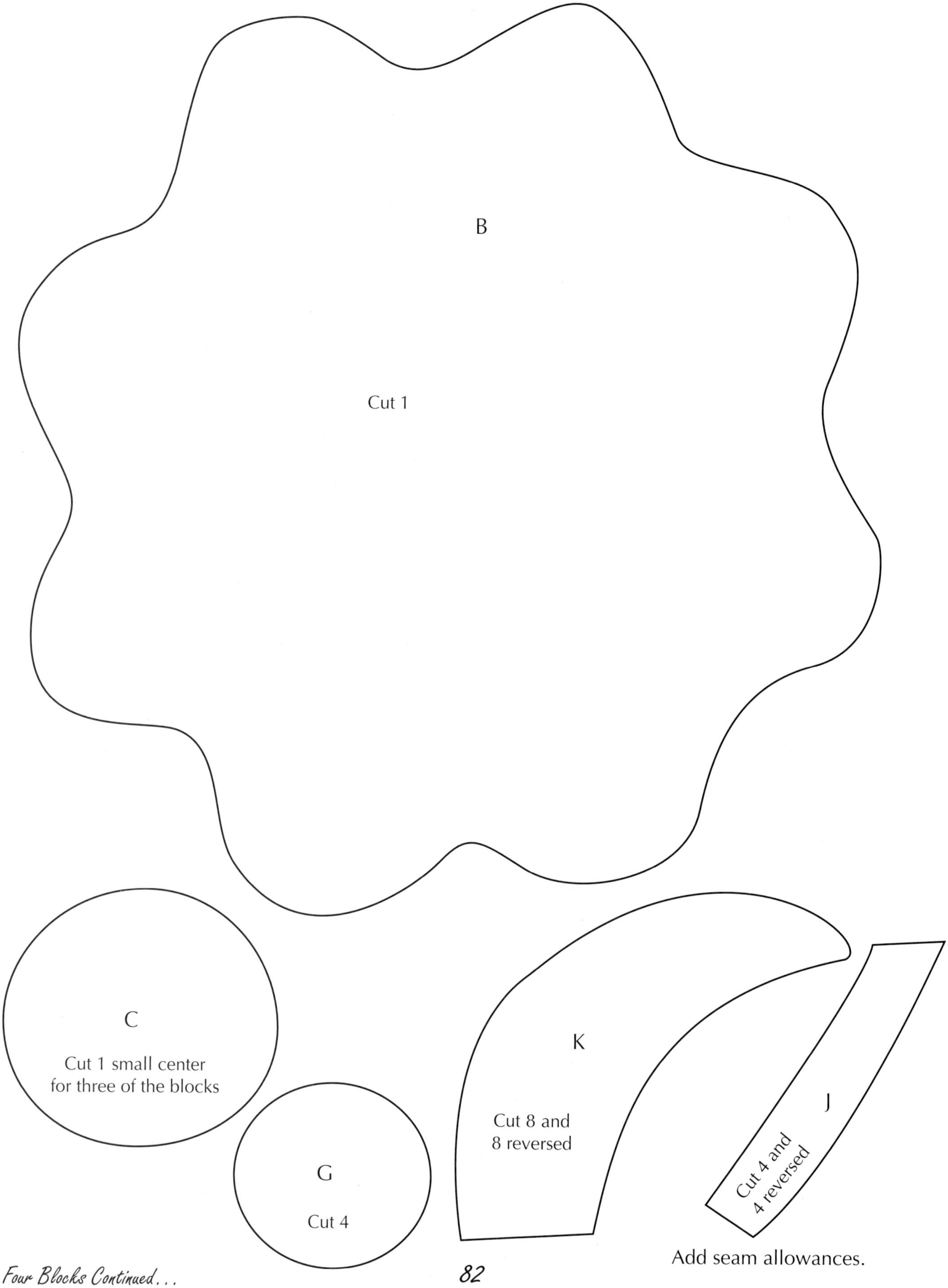
B
Cut 1
C
Cut 1 small center
for three of the blocks
G
Cut 4
K
Cut 8 and
8 reversed
J
Cut 4 and
4 reversed

Add seam allowances.

*Four Blocks Continued...*

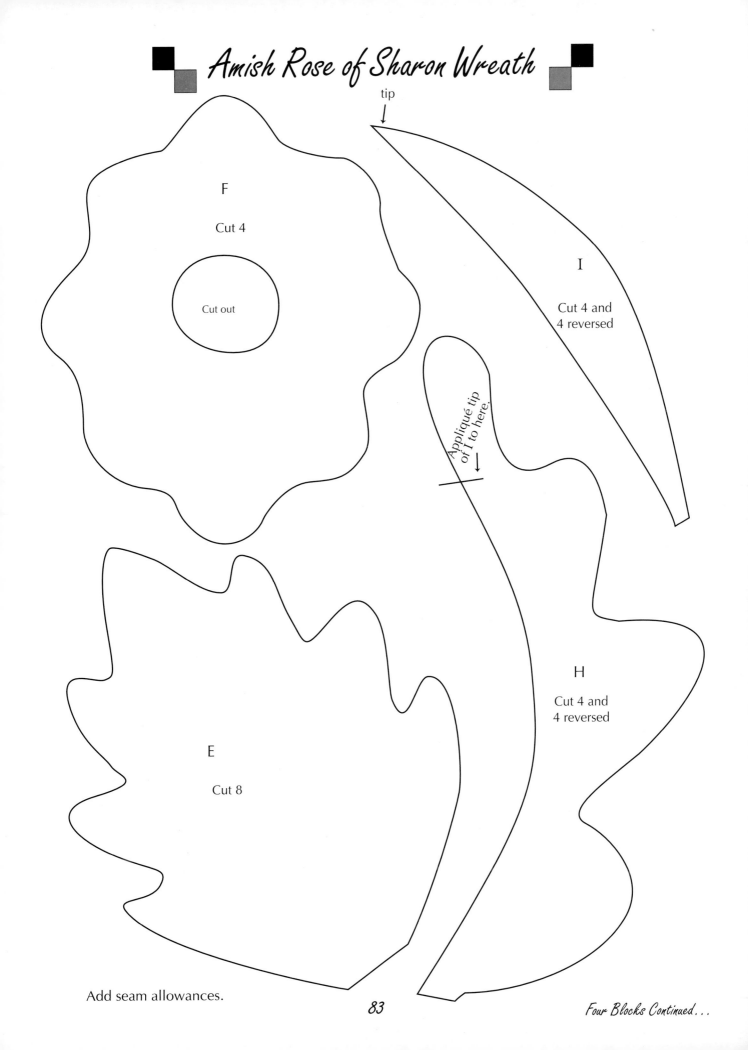

tip

F

Cut 4

Cut out

I

Cut 4 and
4 reversed

Appliqué tip
of I to here.

H

Cut 4 and
4 reversed

E

Cut 8

Add seam allowances.

*Four Blocks Continued . . .*

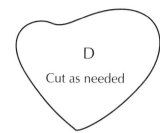

D

Cut as needed

Cut as needed

E

C

Cut as needed

Add seam allowances
to appliqué pieces.

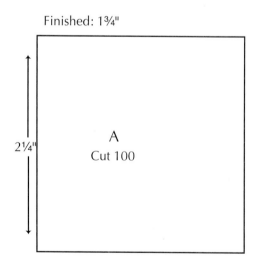

Finished: 1¾"

2¼"

A
Cut 100

2¼"

B
Cut 100

Finished: 1¾"

Seam allowance included.

Tree – Scaled down to 15% of original

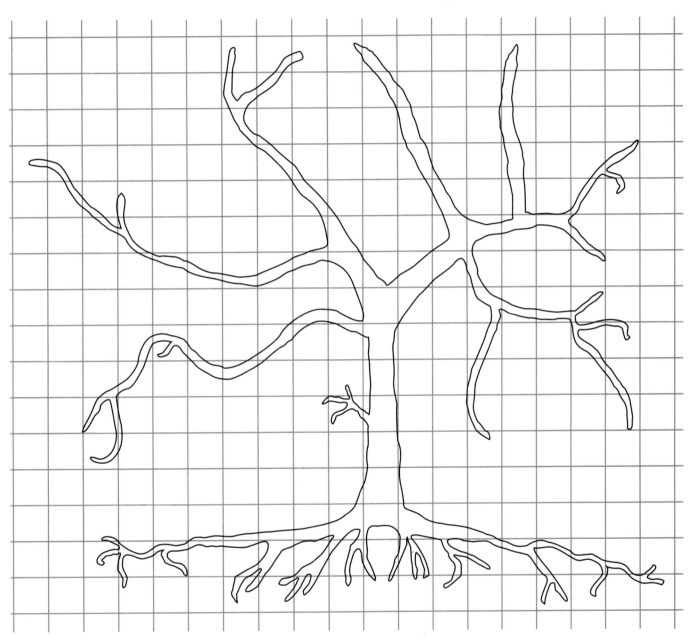

To enlarge the tree pattern, tape paper together to make a 48" square. Draw a grid spacing the lines 2½" apart both vertically and horizontally. You will have 2½" squares covering the paper. Transfer the design, square by square, to prepare the full scale pattern for the quilt.

Add seam allowances.

85

*Four Blocks Continued...*

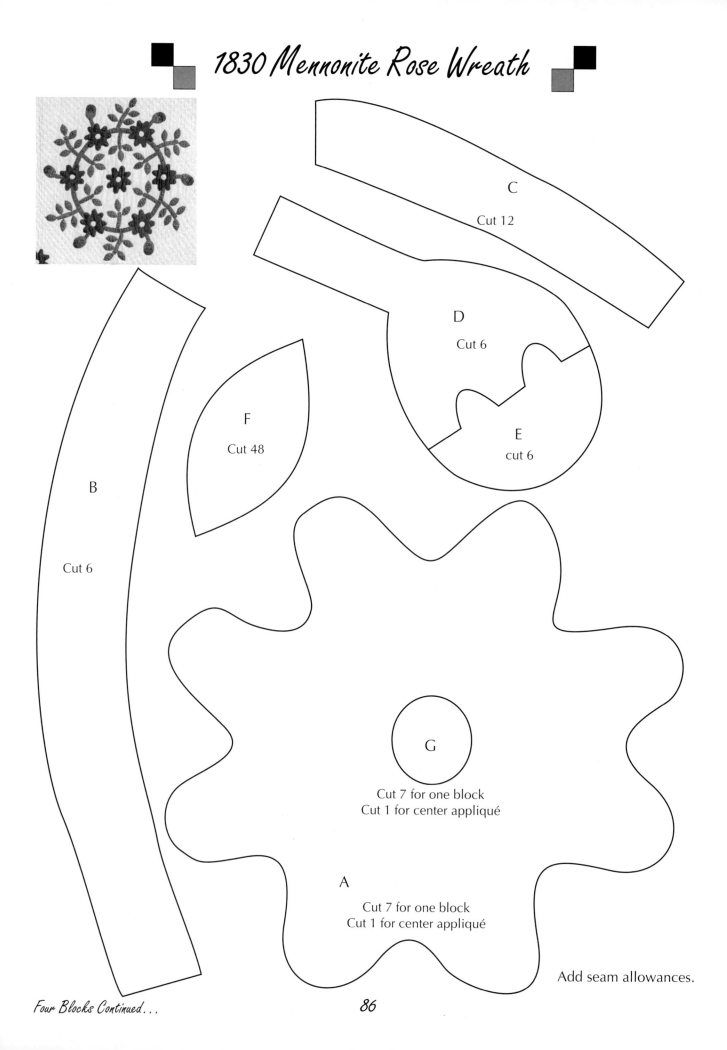

C

Cut 12

D

Cut 6

F

Cut 48

E

cut 6

B

Cut 6

G

Cut 7 for one block
Cut 1 for center appliqué

A

Cut 7 for one block
Cut 1 for center appliqué

Add seam allowances.

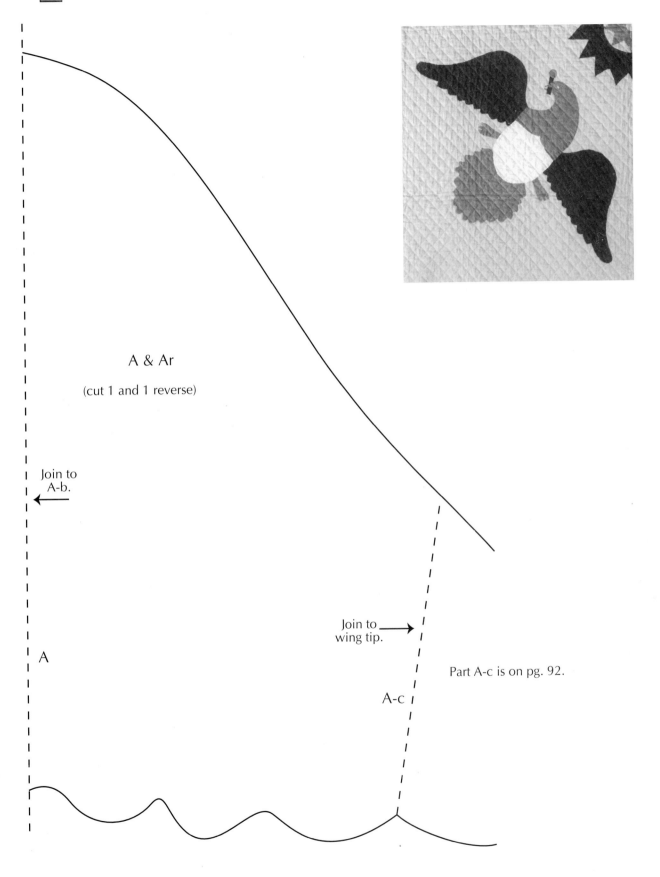

A & Ar

(cut 1 and 1 reverse)

Join to
A-b.
←

A

Join to ⟶
wing tip.

Part A-c is on pg. 92.

A-c

Add seam allowances.

Four Blocks Continued . . .

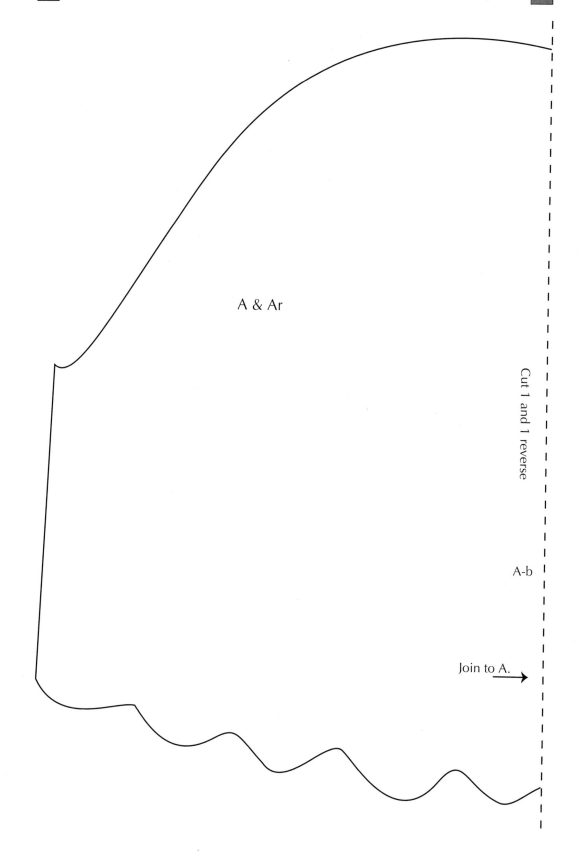

A & Ar

Cut 1 and 1 reverse

A-b

Join to A. →

Add seam allowances.

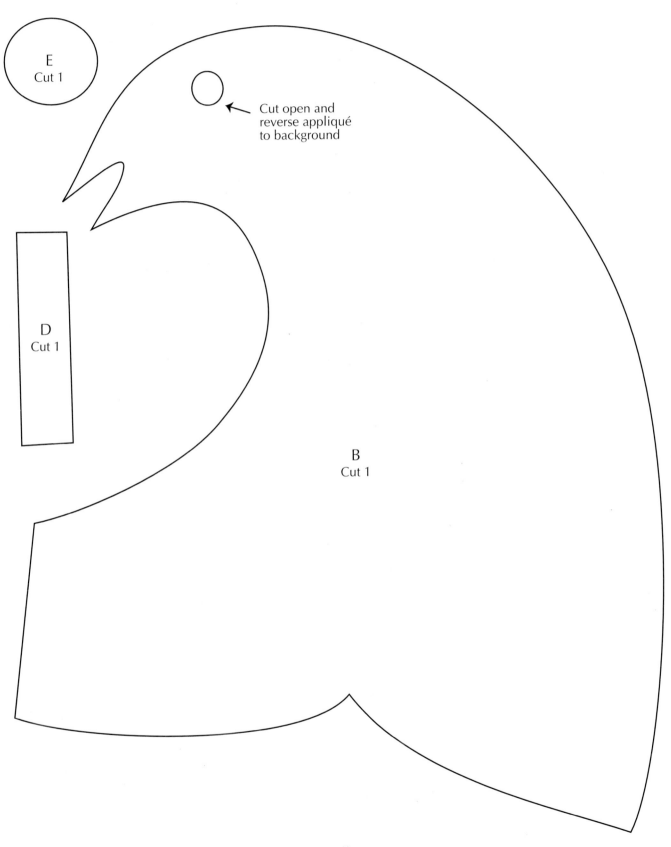

E
Cut 1

Cut open and
reverse appliqué
to background

D
Cut 1

B
Cut 1

Add seam allowances.

*Four Blocks Continued...*

Cut 1
and 1
reverse

F

C

Cut 1

Add seam allowances.

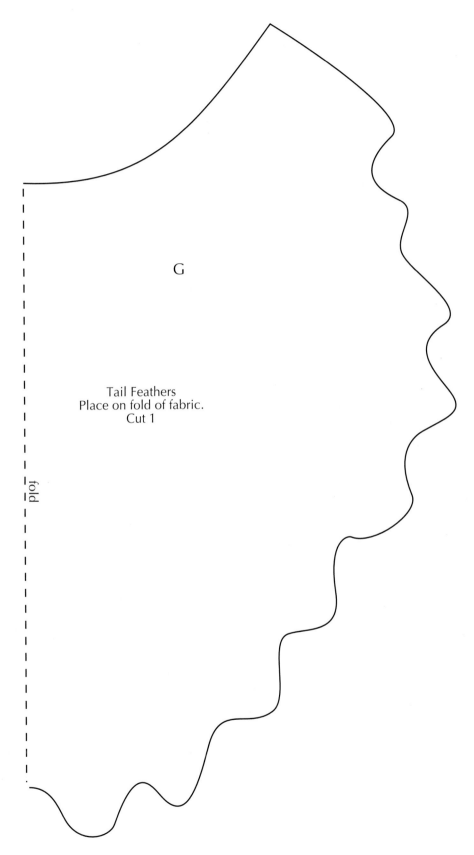

G

Tail Feathers
Place on fold of fabric.
Cut 1

fold

Add seam allowances.

*Four Blocks Continued...*

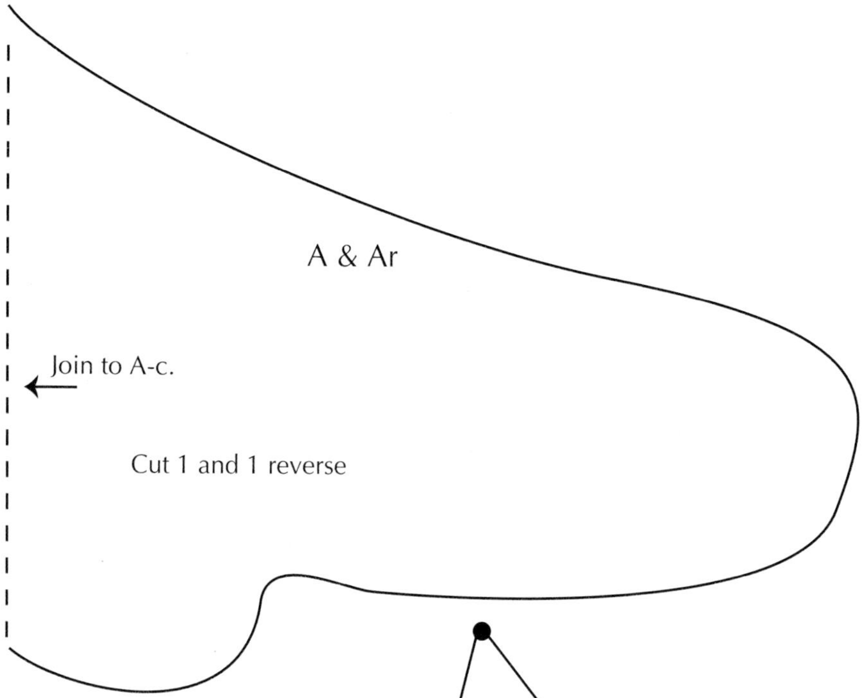

A & Ar

Join to A-c.

Cut 1 and 1 reverse

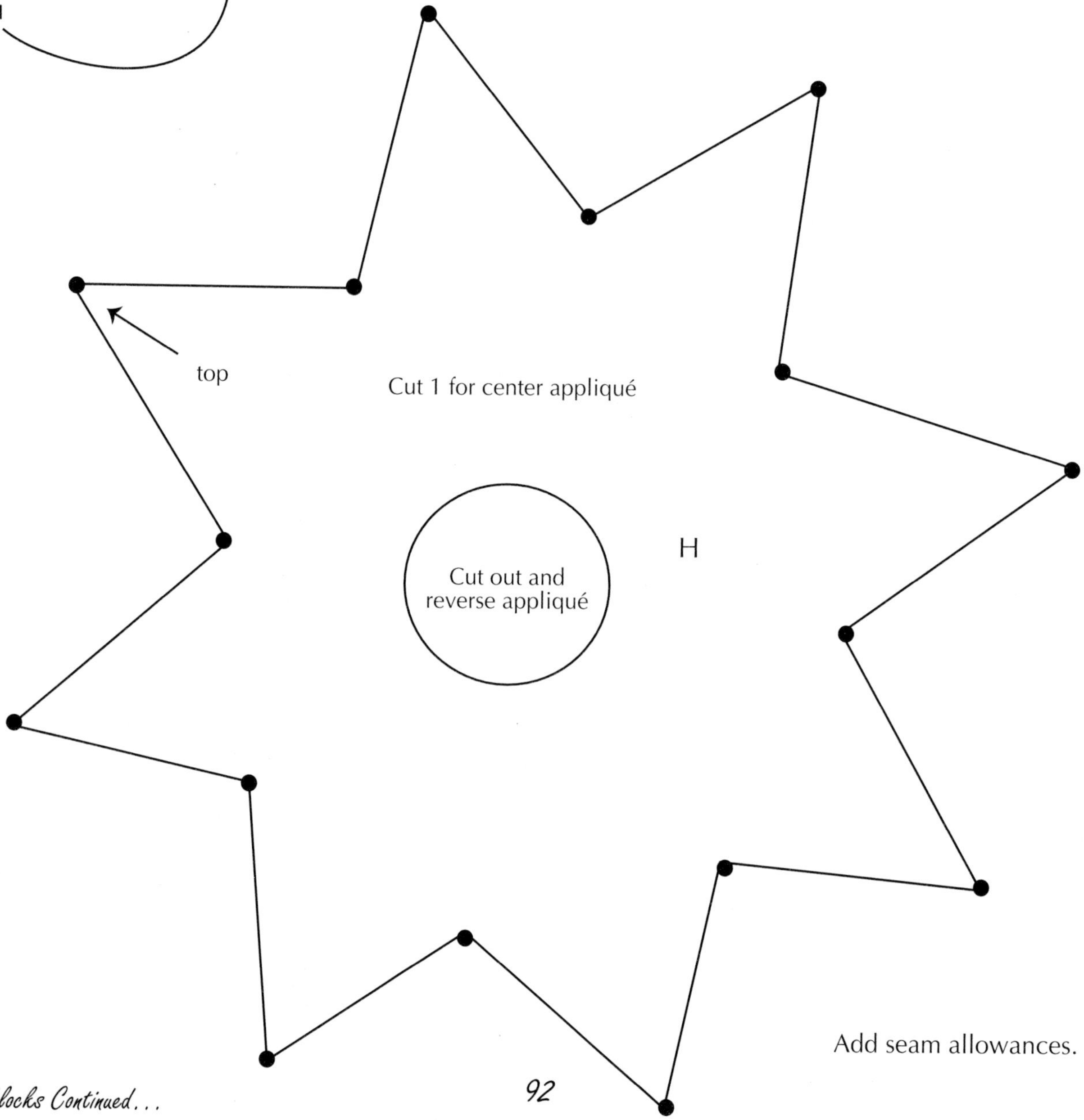

top

Cut 1 for center appliqué

H

Cut out and
reverse appliqué

Add seam allowances.

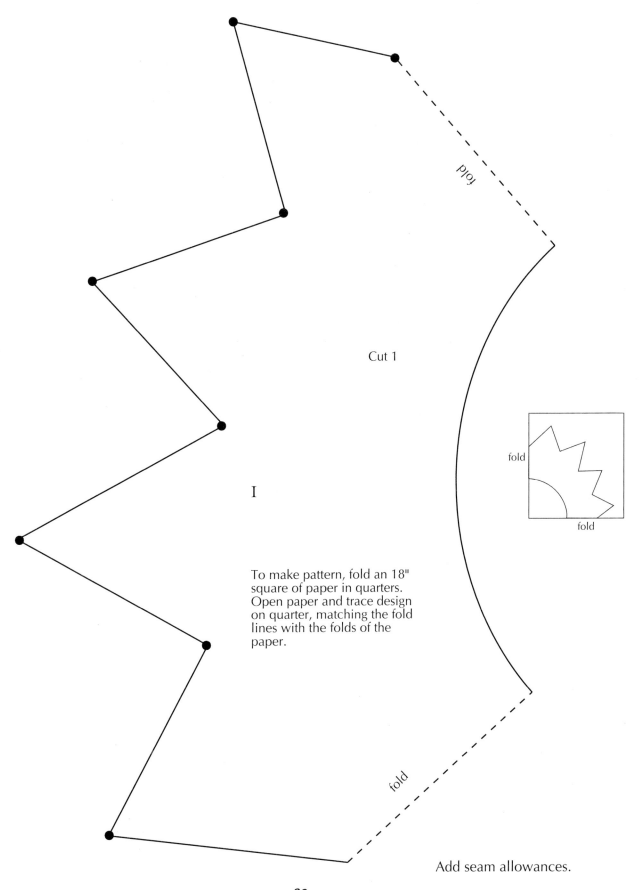

Cut 1

I

fold

fold

To make pattern, fold an 18"
square of paper in quarters.
Open paper and trace design
on quarter, matching the fold
lines with the folds of the
paper.

fold

fold

Add seam allowances.

*Four Blocks Continued . . .*

# Grape Wreaths

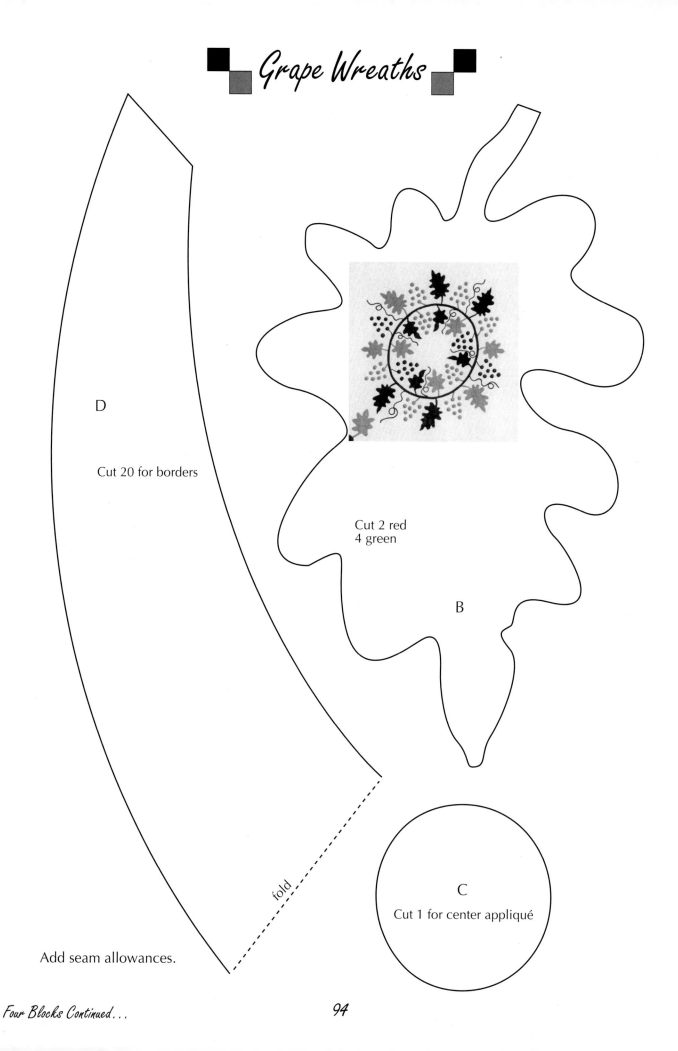

D

Cut 20 for borders

Cut 2 red
4 green

B

fold

Add seam allowances.

C

Cut 1 for center appliqué

# Grape Wreaths

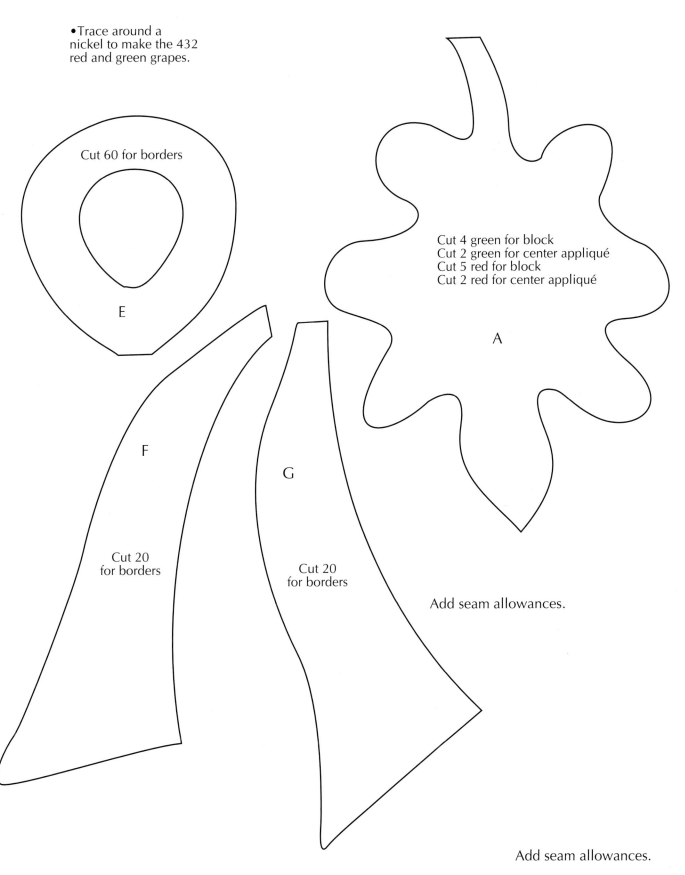

•Trace around a nickel to make the 432 red and green grapes.

Cut 60 for borders

E

Cut 4 green for block
Cut 2 green for center appliqué
Cut 5 red for block
Cut 2 red for center appliqué

A

F

G

Cut 20
for borders

Cut 20
for borders

Add seam allowances.

Add seam allowances.

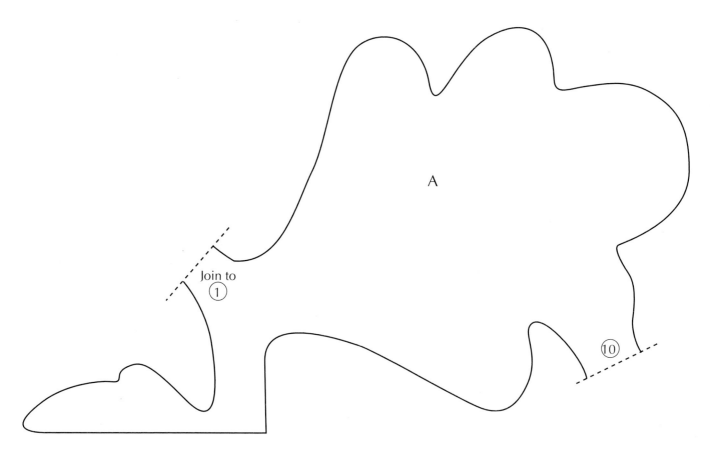

A

Join to
①

⑩

Add seam allowances.

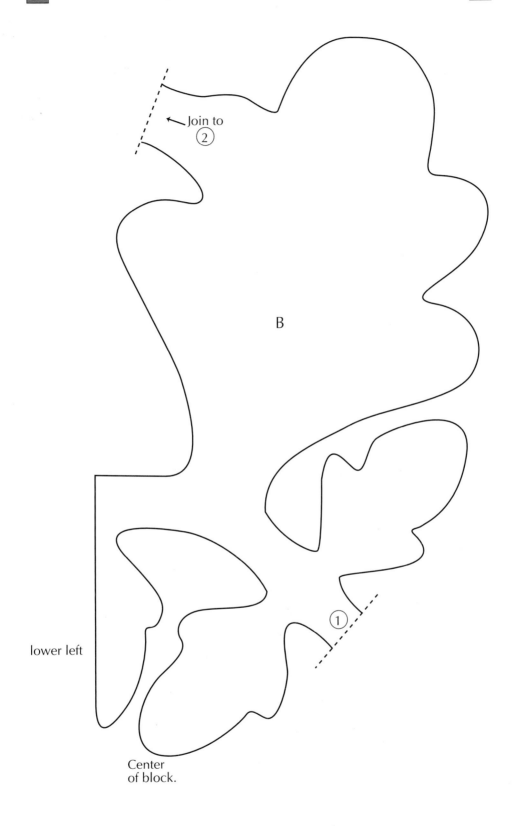

← Join to ②

B

lower left

①

Center
of block.

Add seam allowances.

*Four Blocks Continued...*

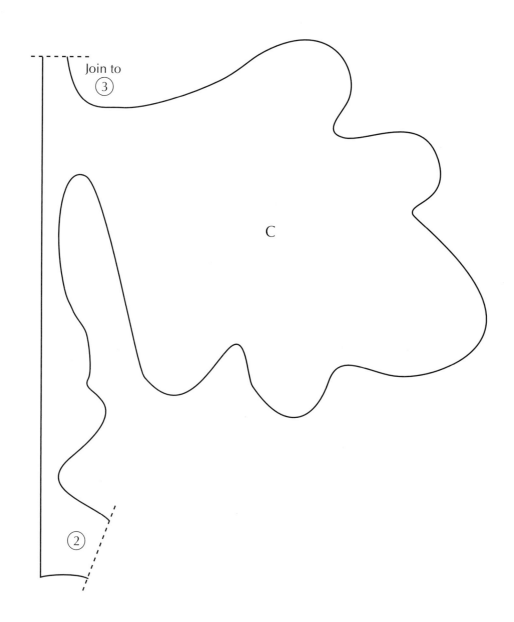

Join to ③

② C

Add seam allowances.

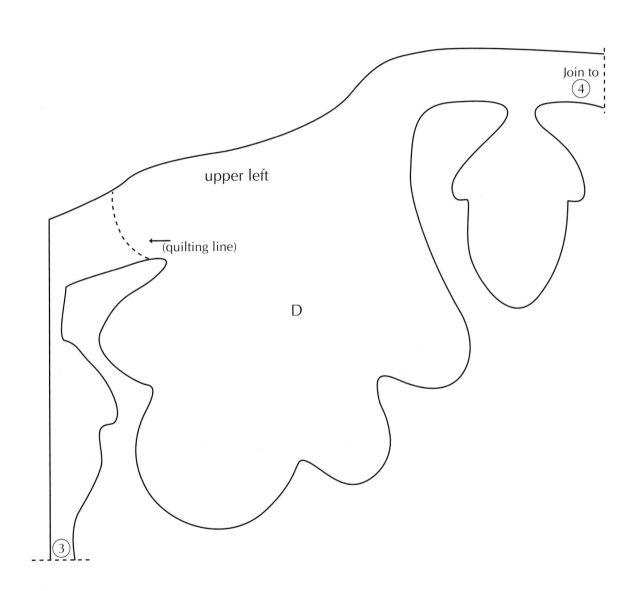

Join to
④

upper left

(quilting line)

D

③

Add seam allowances.

*Four Blocks Continued...*

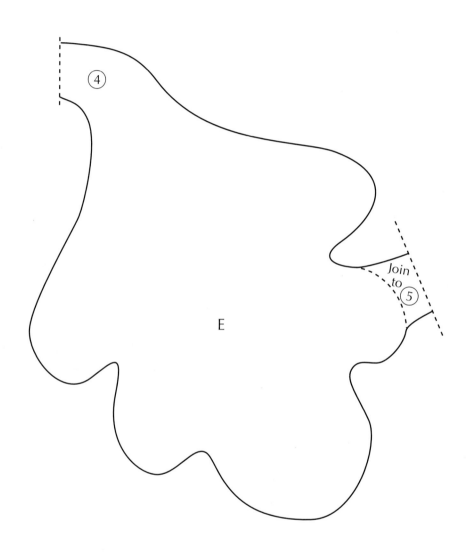

④

Join
to
⑤

E

Add seam allowances.

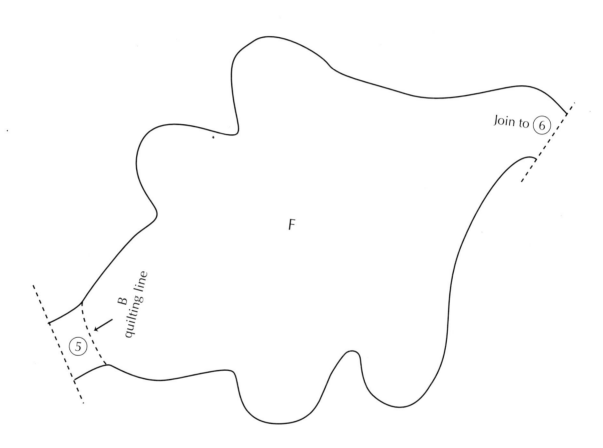

F

Join to ⑥

⑤

B
quilting line

Add seam allowances.

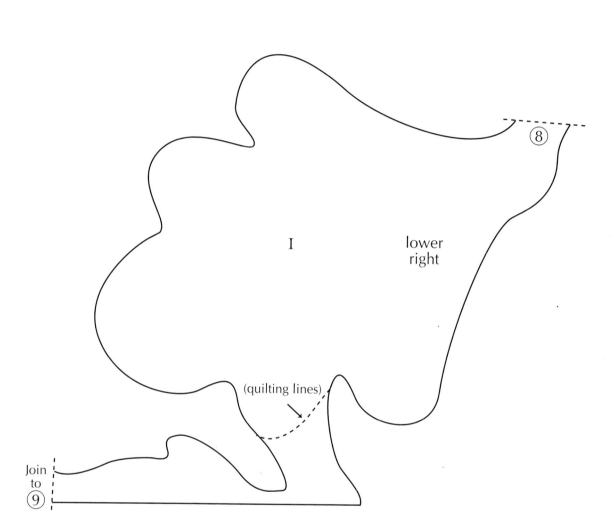

I

lower
right

(quilting lines)

Join
to
⑨

⑧

Add seam allowances.

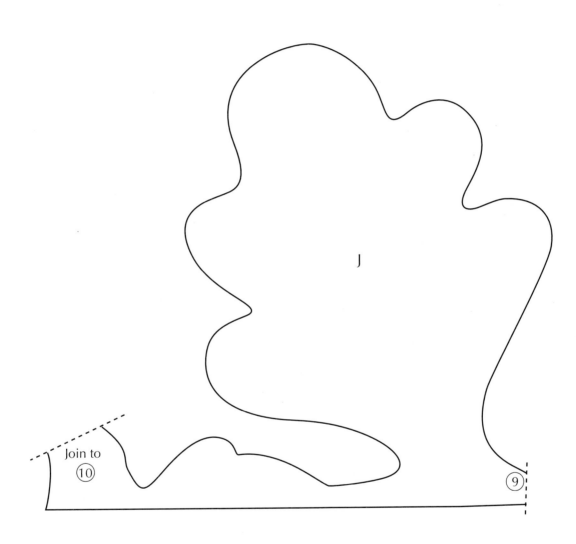

Join to
⑩

⑨

J

Add seam allowances.

*Four Blocks Continued...*

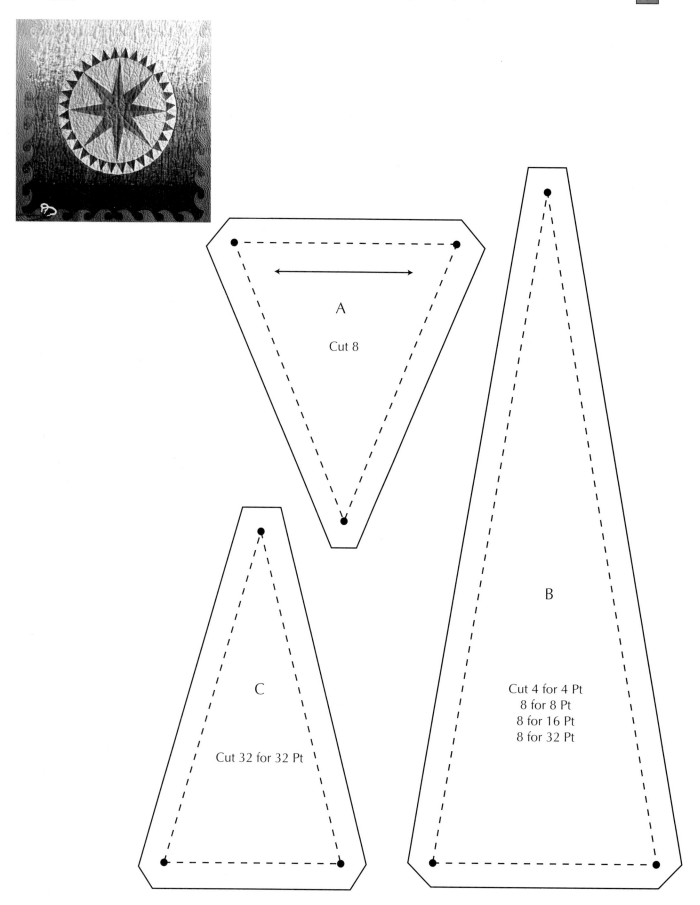

A

Cut 8

B

Cut 4 for 4 Pt
8 for 8 Pt
8 for 16 Pt
8 for 32 Pt

C

Cut 32 for 32 Pt

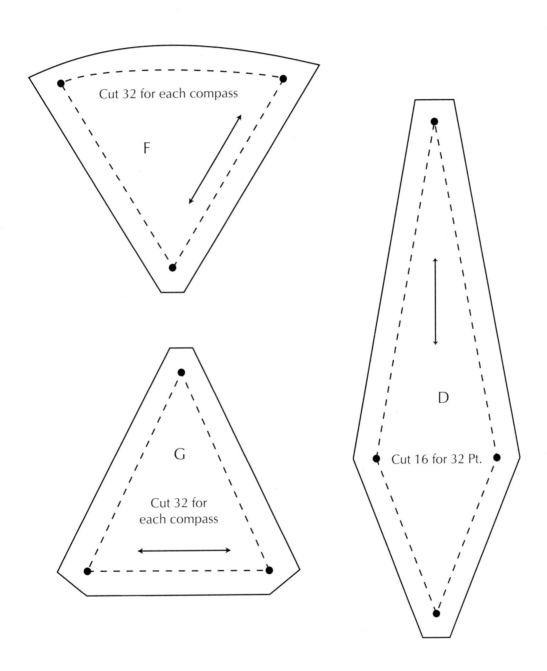

Cut 32 for each compass

F

G

Cut 32 for
each compass

D

Cut 16 for 32 Pt.

*Four Blocks Continued...*

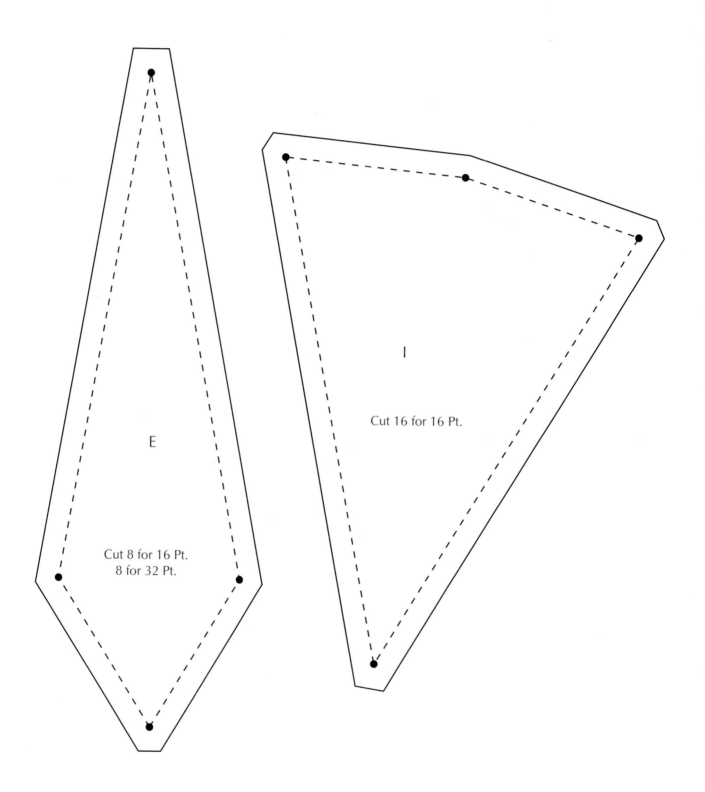

E

Cut 8 for 16 Pt.
8 for 32 Pt.

I

Cut 16 for 16 Pt.

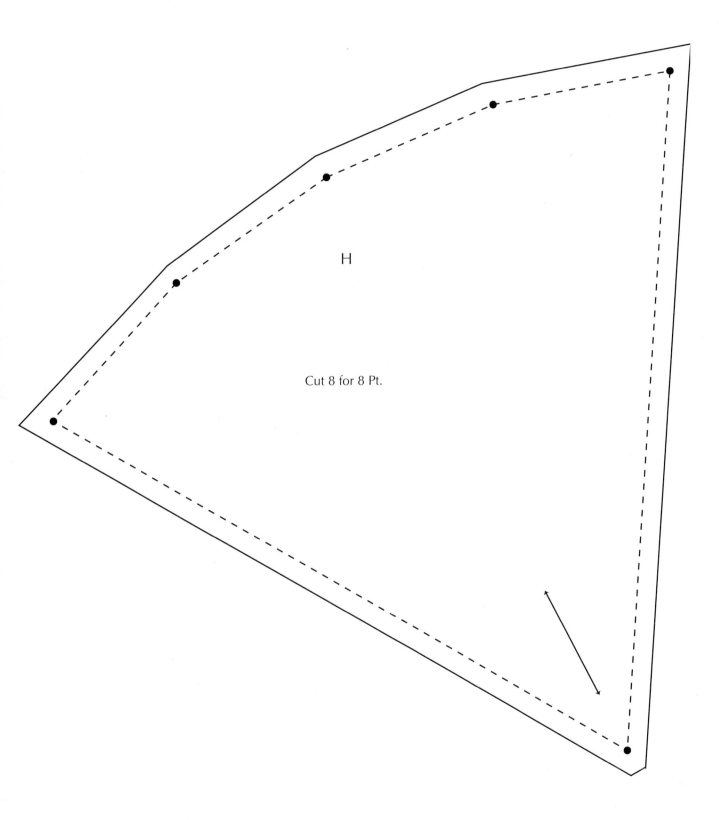

H

Cut 8 for 8 Pt.

*Four Blocks Continued...*

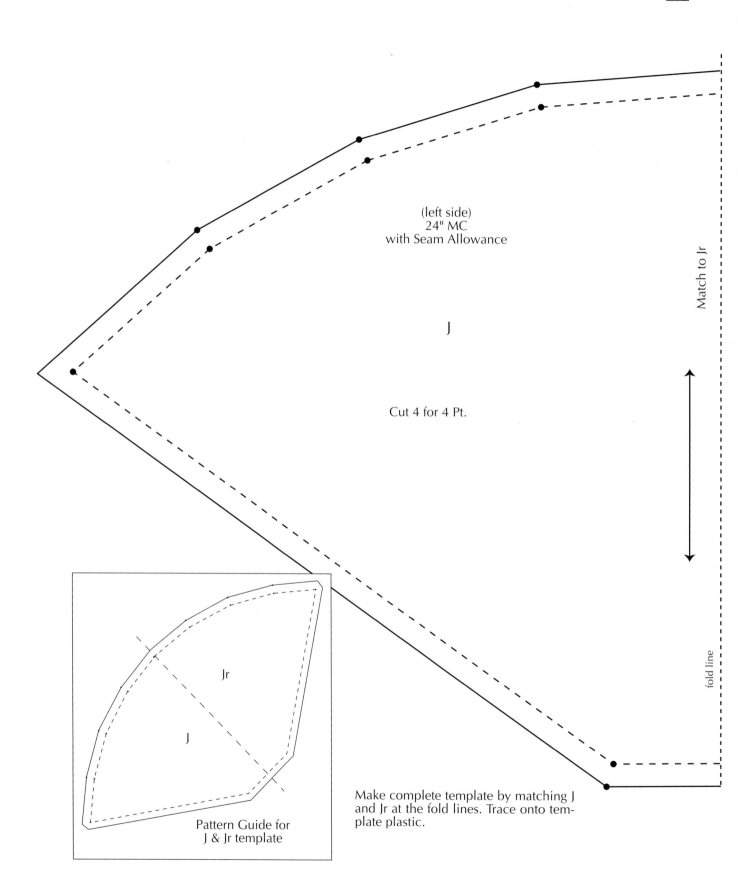

(left side)
24" MC
with Seam Allowance

J

Cut 4 for 4 Pt.

Match to Jr

fold line

Jr

J

Pattern Guide for
J & Jr template

Make complete template by matching J
and Jr at the fold lines. Trace onto template plastic.

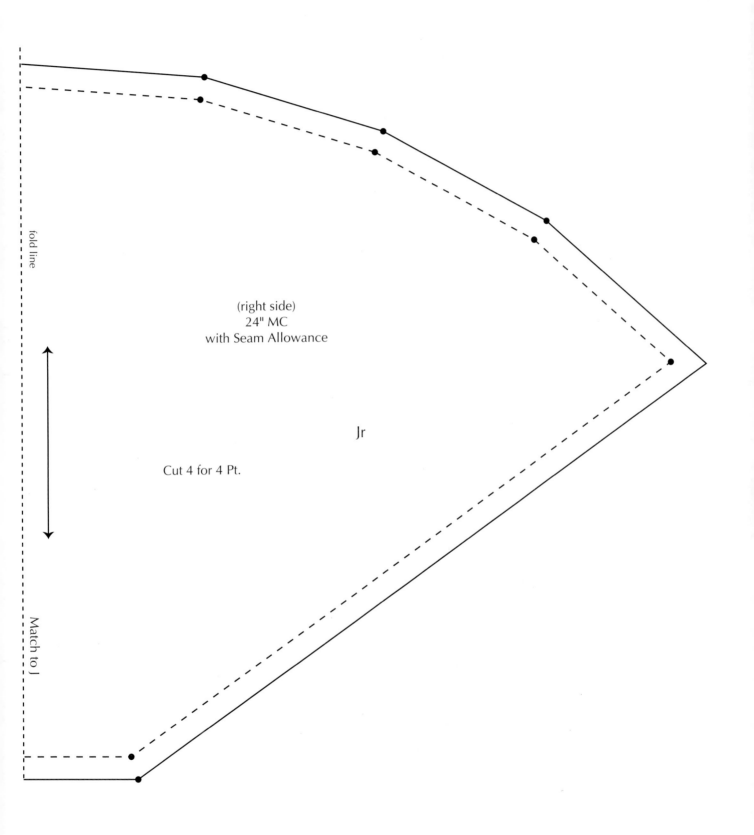

fold line

(right side)
24" MC
with Seam Allowance

Jr

Cut 4 for 4 Pt.

Match to J

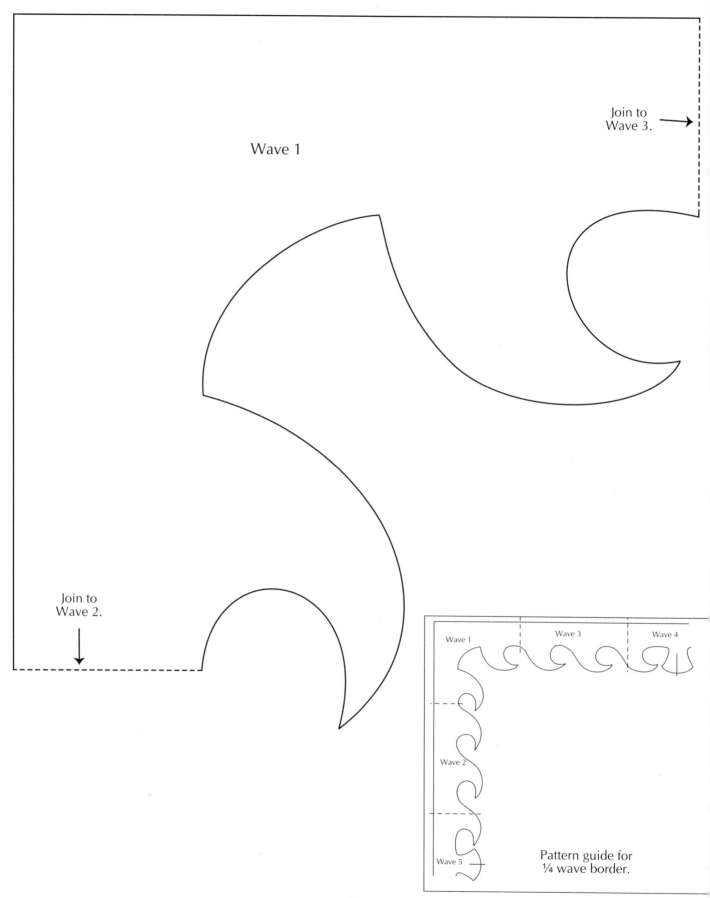

Wave 1

Join to
Wave 3.

Join to
Wave 2.

Wave 1

Wave 3

Wave 4

Wave 2

Wave 5

Pattern guide for
¼ wave border.

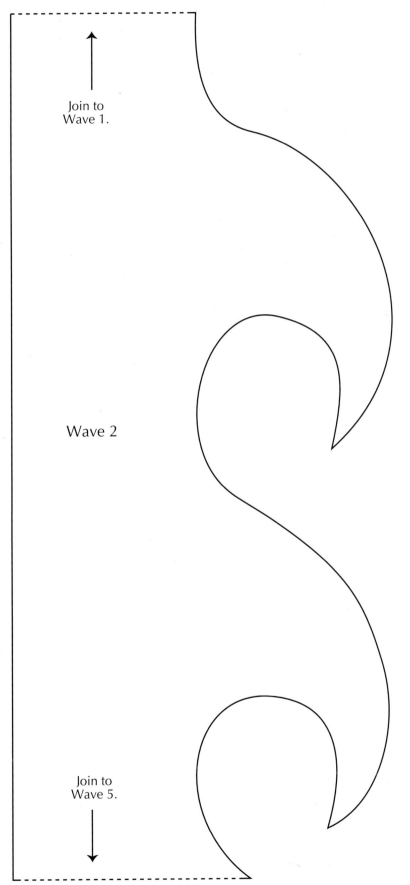

Join to
Wave 1.

Wave 2

Join to
Wave 5.

*Four Blocks Continued...*

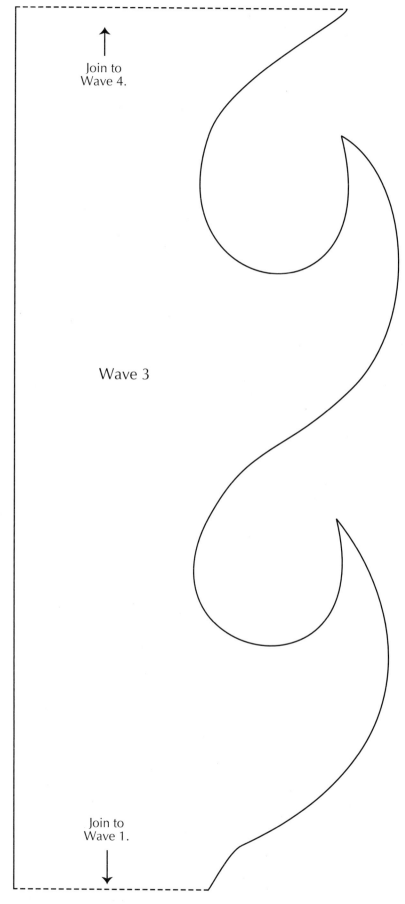

Join to
Wave 4.

Wave 3

Join to
Wave 1.

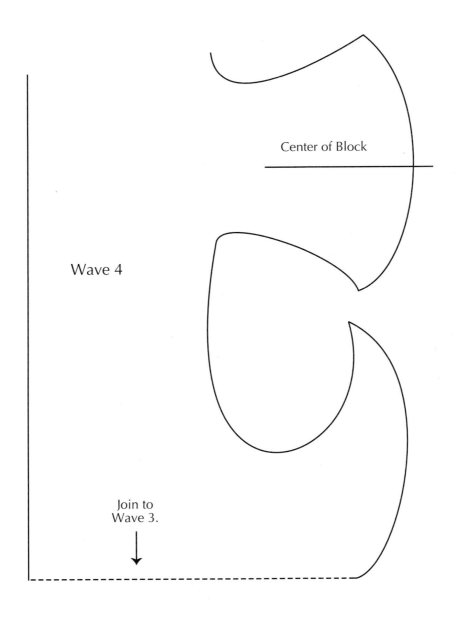

Center of Block

Wave 4

Join to
Wave 3.

*Four Blocks Continued...*

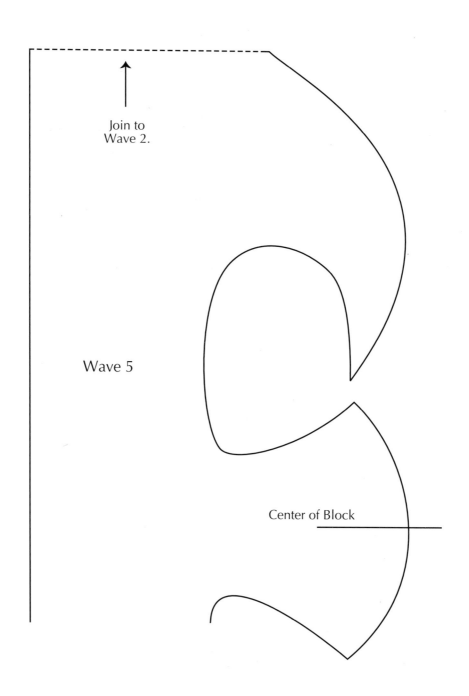

Join to
Wave 2.

Wave 5

Center of Block

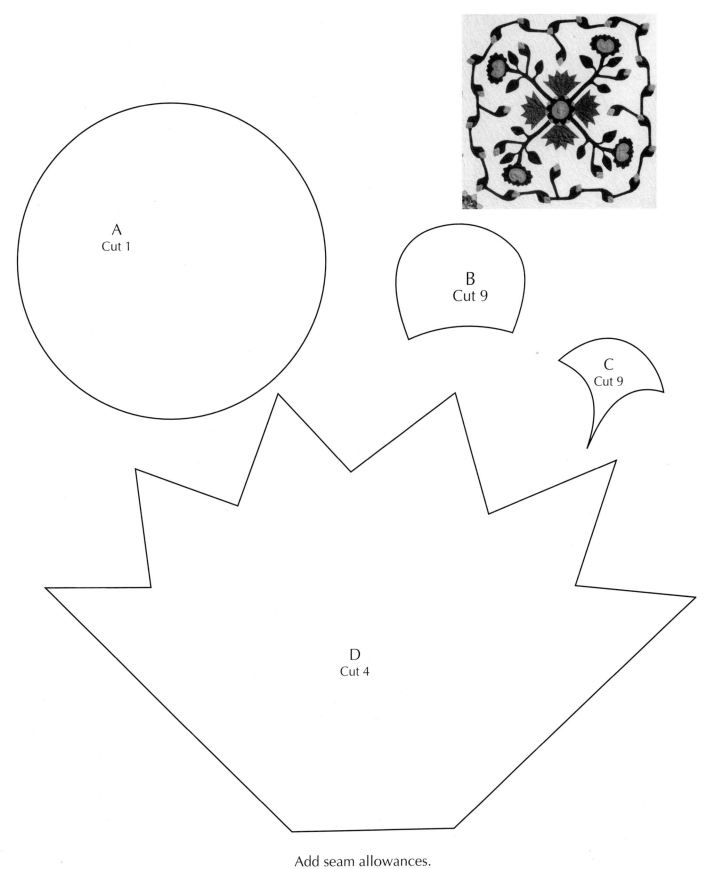

A
Cut 1

B
Cut 9

C
Cut 9

D
Cut 4

Add seam allowances.

Four Blocks Continued...

# Whig-Harrison Rose

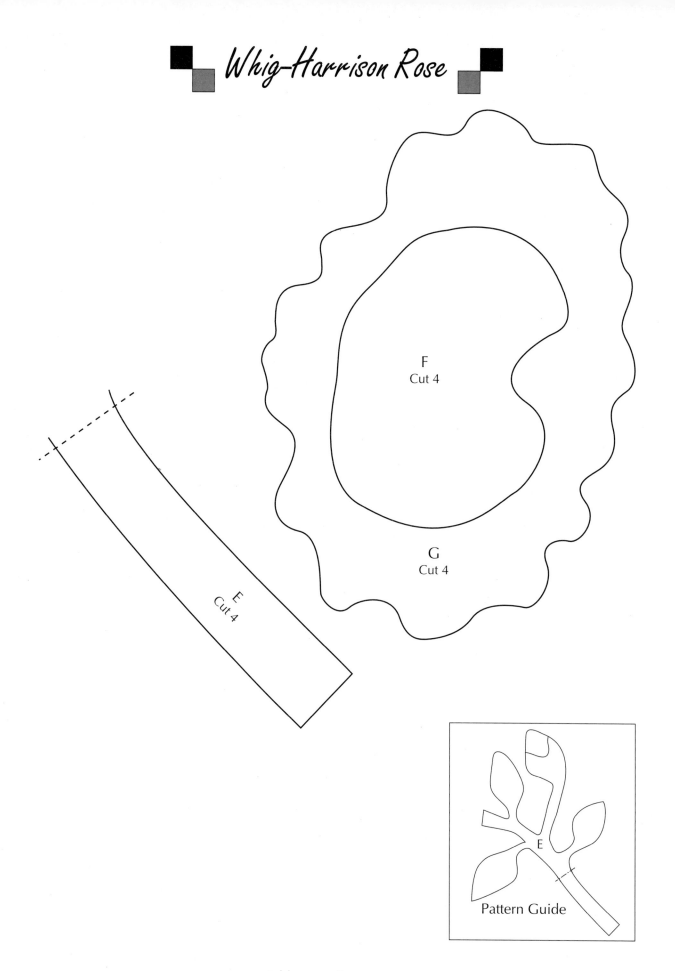

F
Cut 4

G
Cut 4

E
Cut 4

E

Pattern Guide

Add seam allowances.

# Whig-Harrison Rose

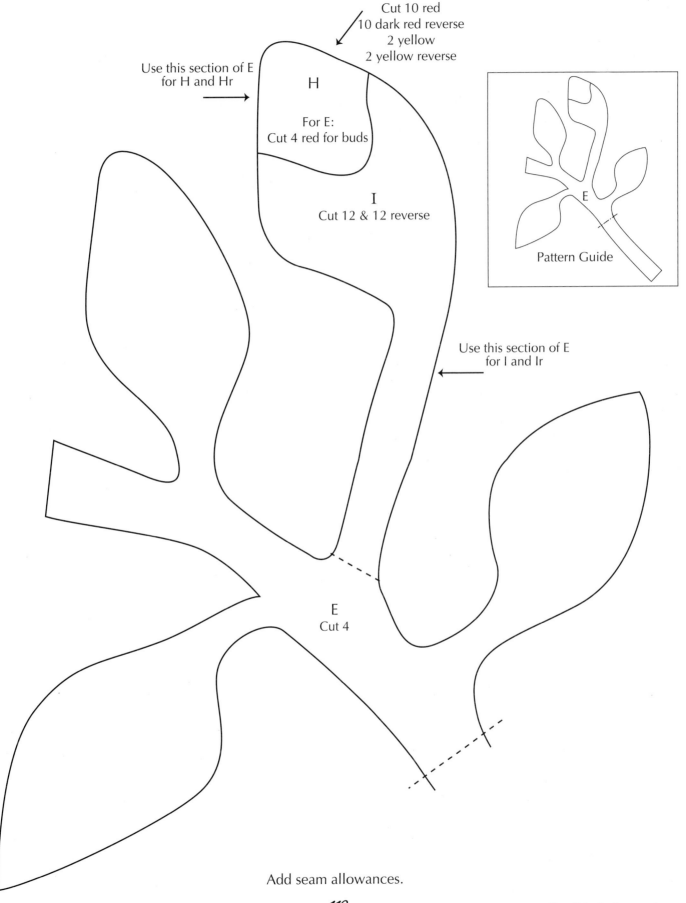

Cut 10 red
10 dark red reverse
2 yellow
2 yellow reverse

Use this section of E
for H and Hr

H

For E:
Cut 4 red for buds

I
Cut 12 & 12 reverse

Pattern Guide

E

Use this section of E
for I and Ir

E
Cut 4

Add seam allowances.

*Four Blocks Continued . . .*

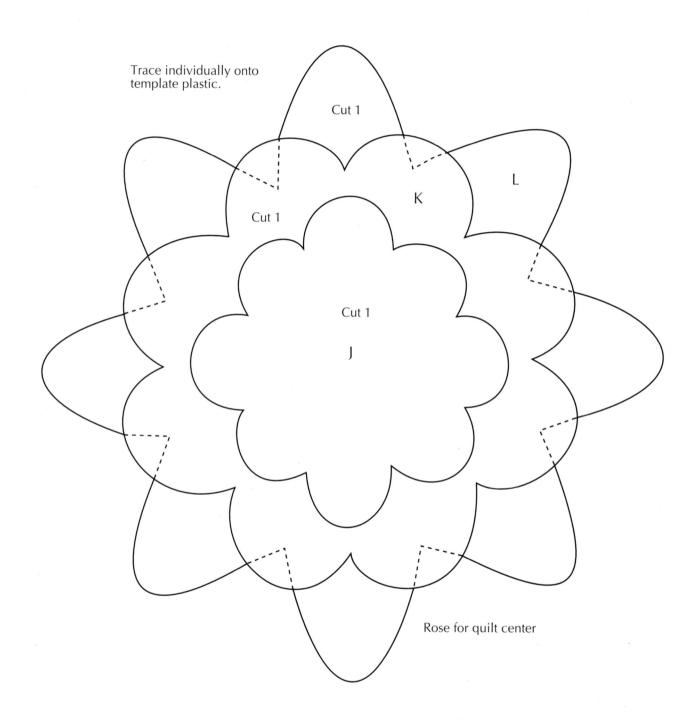

Trace individually onto template plastic.

Cut 1

L

K

Cut 1

Cut 1

J

Rose for quilt center

Add seam allowances.

5" Fan Quilting Template

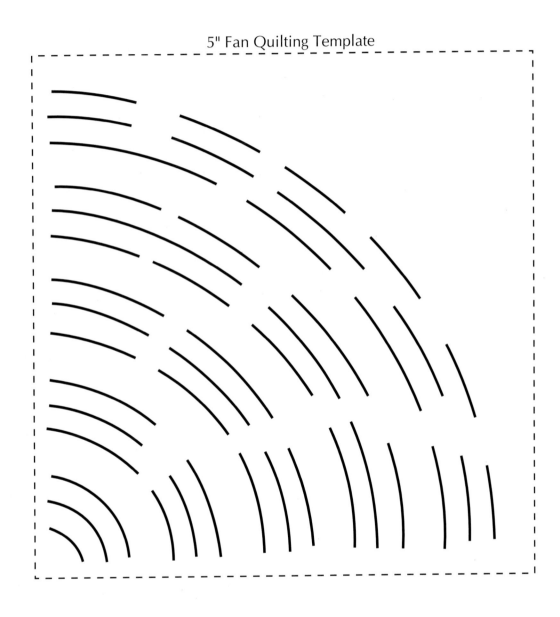

*Four Blocks Continued...*

Cut 1

L

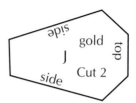

side

gold

top

J

Cut 2

side

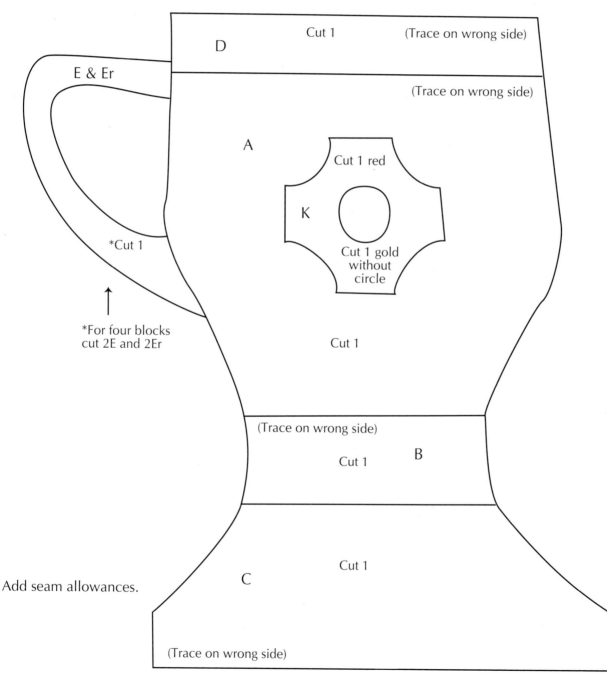

D    Cut 1    (Trace on wrong side)

E & Er

(Trace on wrong side)

A

Cut 1 red

K

Cut 1 gold
without
circle

*Cut 1

Cut 1

↑

*For four blocks
cut 2E and 2Er

(Trace on wrong side)

Cut 1    B

Cut 1

C

Add seam allowances.

(Trace on wrong side)

*Four Blocks Continued . . .*

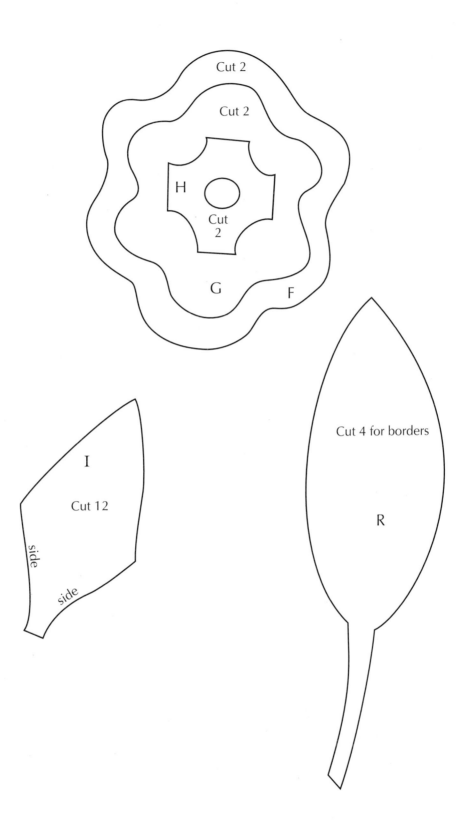

Cut 2

Cut 2

H

Cut 2

G

F

I

Cut 12

side

side

Cut 4 for borders

R

Add seam allowances.

123

*Four Blocks Continued...*

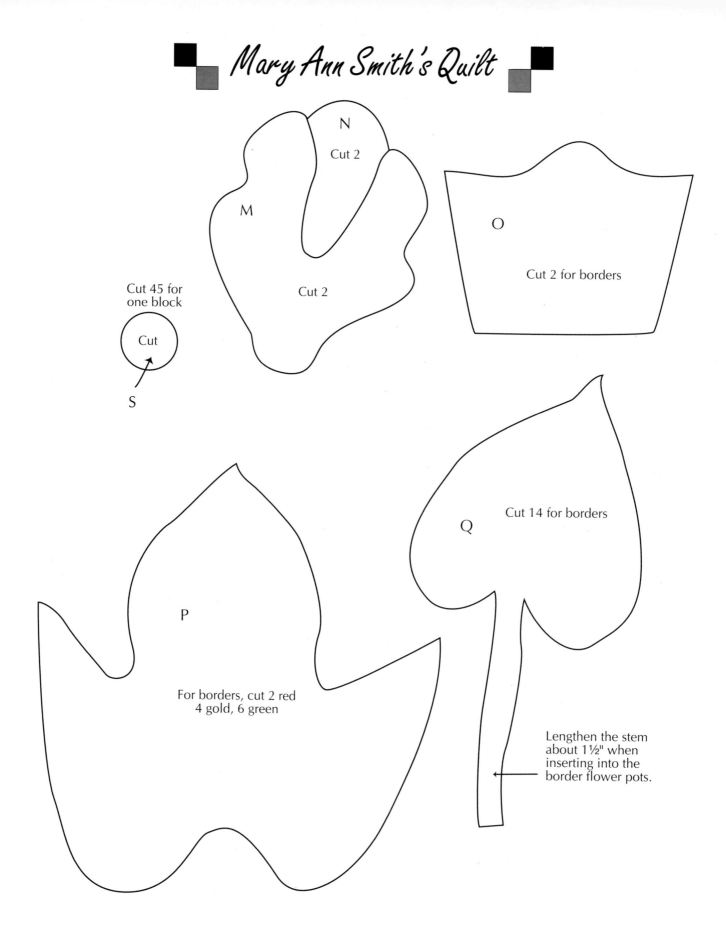

N

Cut 2

M

Cut 2

Cut 45 for
one block

Cut

S

O

Cut 2 for borders

P

For borders, cut 2 red
4 gold, 6 green

Q

Cut 14 for borders

Lengthen the stem
about 1½" when
inserting into the
border flower pots.

Add seam allowances.

Start mark at right end
of top and bottom borders.
On side borders, first
measure 10" from the
right end, then start marking.
Stop 10" from end of side
borders.

Guideline for the bias
serpentine vine.

end of 11½" section

Add seam allowances.

*Four Blocks Continued...*

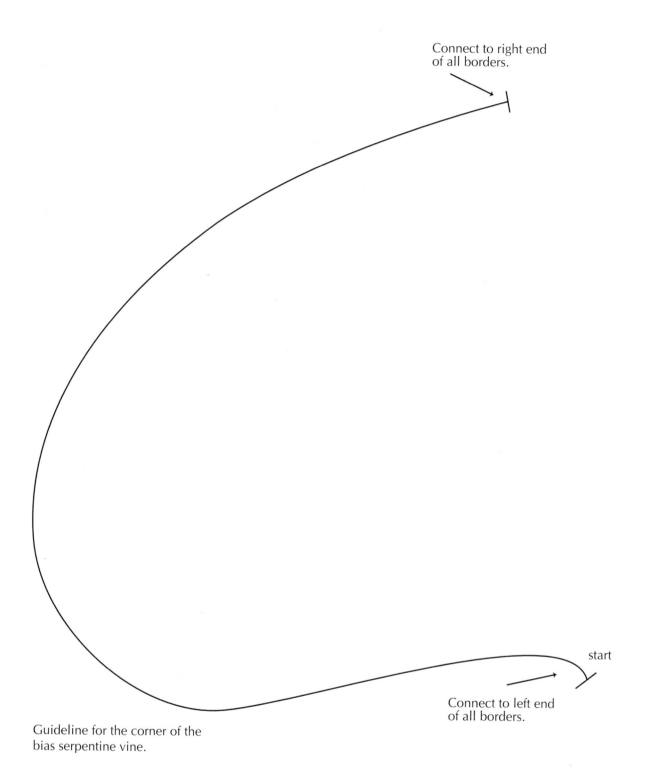

Connect to right end
of all borders.

start

Connect to left end
of all borders.

Guideline for the corner of the
bias serpentine vine.

Add seam allowances.

# About the Author

## Linda Giesler Carlson

Since the 1980s, Linda has taught in all areas of quilting, turning to appliqué and the history and techniques of making the large four-block quilts in the latter part of the decade. She has taught across the country for guilds, retreats, symposiums, and large quilt shows, including the AQS Quilt Show. Her work has been featured in several quilting magazines and books, and her first book, *Roots, Feathers & Blooms: 4-Block Quilts, Their History & Patterns, Book I*, was published by the American Quilter's Society in 1994.

As a result of her extensive research, Linda was invited to present a paper, "The Roots of the Large Four Block Quilt" for the What's American About American Quilts? symposium at the Smithsonian Institution, Washington D.C., in 1995.

In the summer of 1997, Linda's collection of antique and new original four-block quilts was exhibited at the Museum of the American Quilter's Society, Paducah, Kentucky.

Linda and her family reside in Mexico, Missouri, where she continues her research on four-block quilts. In 1996 she received the G. Andy Runge Ambassador Award in recognition of her representation of her hometown during her many travels and teaching experiences.

*Four Blocks Continued...*

# AQS BOOKS ON QUILTS

This is only a partial listing of the books on quilts that are available from the American Quilter's Society. AQS books are known the world over for their timely topics, clear writing, beautiful color photographs, and accurate illustrations and patterns. Most of the following books are available from your local bookseller, quilt shop, or public library. If you are unable to locate certain titles in your area, you may order by mail from the AMERICAN QUILTER'S SOCIETY, P.O. Box 3290, Paducah, KY 42002-3290. Customers with Visa or MasterCard may phone in orders from 7:00–5:00 CST, Monday–Friday, Toll Free 1-800-626-5420. Add $2.00 for postage for the first book ordered and $0.40 for each additional book. Include item number, title, and price when ordering. Allow 14 to 21 days for delivery.